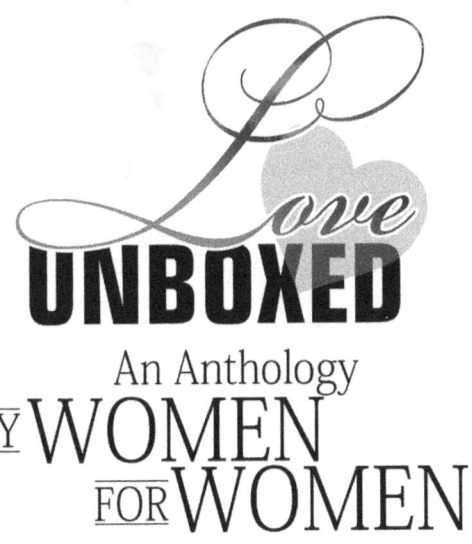

Love UNBOXED

An Anthology BY WOMEN FOR WOMEN

Compiled and Published by

Placida Acheru
WITH A COLLECTION OF HEART-SEARCHING TRANSFORMATIONAL WOMEN

http://bookprojects.uk

Love Unboxed Book 2 copyright © 2017 Placida Acheru and contributing authors

First published as a collection November 2017

ISBN-13: 978-0995734968 (eBook)
ISBN-13: 978-0995734975 (Paperback)

Cover design by Robert Nimako Brefo

All Rights Reserved.

No part of this book may be reproduced in any form or by any electronic or mechanical means, including storage and retrieval systems, without written permission from the publisher, except in the case of a reviewer, who may quote brief passages embodied in critical articles or in a review.

The publisher does not have any control over and does not assume any responsibility for author or third-party websites and their content.

Disclaimer

This book is to educate and provide general information. The reader is advised to consult with their advisor regarding their specific situation. The author and compiler has taken reasonable precautions in the preparation of this book and believes that the facts presented were accurate at the time of writing. The author and compiler does not assume any responsibility for error or omissions. The author and compiler specifically disclaim any liability resulting from the use or application of the information contained in the book.

Book Projects proudly features writers from all over the English-speaking world. Some speak and write English as their first language, while for others, it's their second, third or even fourth language. Naturally, across all versions of English, there are differences in punctuation and spelling, and even in meaning. These differences are reflected in the work Book Projects publishes, and it accounts for any differences in punctuation, spelling and meaning found within these pages.

PRAISE FOR LOVE UNBOXED

Much more than a romantic novel. In ´*Love Unboxed*´ you´ll read incredible love stories that marked the lives of different women. Enter a vortex of passion and desire that will captivate you from the first line. Each personal story could be your own, your unique fantasy or perhaps, a restrained woman yet to be discovered. Live a unique literary experience from the hands of these women writers who will guide you to your own identity: The adventure of being a woman.

-Victoria Calvo: Author of Independence Ties. A novel about an indomitable woman who fought in the War of Independence.

Not every day one finds a book full of life. Books are written to induce people to imagine, find fantasy worlds full of characters and recreated stories, worlds that take them to unthinkable places. *Love Unboxed* will invite you to take a journey to the most remote places of your being, it will drive you through truth to the best place one can find: The empowerment of love.

Every story told in this marvellous book tells the initiation journey, the life story of women who fight, who live, who work, who feel, who transform love into the greatest tool of massive construction that exists.

Without a shadow of a doubt, a unique experience that will not leave you unmoved.

-Jose' Luis Fuentes: CEO AlientaCoaching, Master Coach, Writer, International Speaker.

In this book are true examples of a wholehearted life's, where the passion for self-love and the wish to benefit others is evident. Their shared experiences are beautifully inspirational, illustrating how one can be found in toxic relationships only to find that one has a choice, to let go of all the preconceived concepts we are fed and the conditional ways of relating, and to realise that everything we need is right here within us—in, of, as and through Love.

-Madalena Alberto: Singer and West End actress (Evita, Cats) madalenaalberto.com

'Love Unboxed' is a beautiful collection of heart-felt stories from women who show courage, vulnerability and insights and in doing so learn to grow into making better choices and speaking their truth. This book illustrates women perfect in their imperfections having the capacity to transform challenging experiences to serve as guidance in the future, not shackles of their past.

This book will encourage women everywhere and give them the strength to acknowledge the inner voice they must trust in their own discernment & their great capacity for total restoration, no matter how wounded they have been.

It's a fantastic read!

-Natalie Ledwell: Best Selling Author and Co-Founder of Mind Movies LLC.

DEDICATION

This book is dedicated to the women who have inspired me through their acts of bravery.

To Aunt Peggy, who transformed her life from zero to hero. From you I learned the importance of financial independence and leaving a legacy for your children. If you can see it, you can achieve it.

To Lady Comfort Ohia, a woman who overcame the turbulence of marriage by sticking to her marital vows for the sake of her children and the man she loved. I am in awe of your strength, courage and wisdom.

To *Colette Tate* aged eighty-three, who looked after her first husband through twenty years of heart-breaking illness, for him to die at aged sixty-one, then after having not being on a plane since her honeymoon, flying to Tasmania over ten thousand miles away, learning to ski at seventy-two and remarrying at seventy-five, to now be touring the world with her new man.

This dedication would not be complete without mentioning ***Monica Acheru***, my mother. At seventeen married, and after four children almost lost my father, to another woman. She kept her faith in God, praying for twelve years that he would return, and return he did. They are now still together today for a total of fifty-one years.

Whatever your story, the key lesson is to find strength in those around you at times of your weakness. Despair will suffocate you. Love and hope will empower you.

FOREWORD
BY IRMA KURTZ

To fall in love is one side-effect of being human. Falling in love can be a blessing, and it can be a disaster. We all know cases when the blaze of blinding light generated by the fall into love subsides into lifelong warmth between a pair of partners. But as often as not, we all know for ourselves that the fall into love happening as it almost always does by accident on what one writer in the collection calls *"A Rough Road"* can leave its victim with a broken heart in the debris of shattered hope. *Love Unboxed* is a collection of true stories that are every bit as engaging as fiction tries to be when it deals with the topic of love. The stories are told by women, each of whom endured at least one serious fall into love before finally emerging from her recuperation with hope restored by wisdom and a mended heart that is happier than ever before. Although each writer tells us how she managed to climb up out of the chasm and stand in sunshine again, referring to this work as an "advice manual" would denigrate the special tones of the essayists and the music of their voices in chorus. One point of interest, too, is that the harmony of these tales arises from the voices of women who live in various parts of the big world, including those where ancient traditions and parental controls are geared to prevent girls falling into love that has not been prearranged by their elders. The stories span age groups too, thus more than one of them reminisces on maternal love which is, after all, the result of sexual love and remains a version of love to be felt only by females.

Love Unboxed is about love, yes, and it is also a work of love that wants its readers to benefit. Being more than just a good read, the collection offers an important revelation with which every tale in its own way concludes: falling in love delivers a woman into the partnership which she believes deep down to be the one that she deserves. And so, these tales are presented in evidence that for a woman to find herself falling out of love with a disappointing or abusive partner is often as not the result of low self-esteem that made her fall for him in the first place. *"Dreams are Made of Love"* is the title of one in this collection of stories. And does it not also go without saying that love is made of dreams? No two human beings ever dream precisely the same dreams. Each of us makes her own dreams deriving from a part of herself which is all too often shut back into darkness as soon as she is awake again. But feeling and thinking can be joined within one person, and only when that happens will her dreams be seen and achievable, too, by daylight. Thus, do the tales in *Love Unboxed* illustrate that for a woman's meeting with Mister Wonderful to be a blessing, she needs first to meet herself. And before a partner can hold her in respectful affection she must first respect herself. And for the love of another to be the hoped-for voyage of joyful discovery, the first person a woman should love is herself.

- Irma Kurtz, Author, Journalist, Self-help writer. Best known for her column as Agony Aunt at Cosmopolitan for over 40 years.

TABLE OF CONTENTS

Foreword by Irma Kurtz ix

Introduction xv

Part One: Passion, Romance, Fairy Tale 1

   1. Placida Acheru - Courageous women.................................. 2

   2. Christina Tindle - Adventure healing.................................. 6

   3. Chantal Edie N - When all hope is lost............................. 19

   4. Ify Ojo - Taking chances... 31

   5. Gema Ramírez - Prince or Frog... 44

Part Two: Self Discovery, Self-Love and Hope 59

   1. Jenessa Qua - Slimspiration: Losing dead weight........... 60

   2. Luna Miller - To find the way home................................. 73

   3. Christine Smith - Foodie in the making........................... 83

   4. Dr Arinola Araba - What size?... 96

   5. Kimberly Armstrong - Rainbow behind the clouds 110

Part Three: Patience, Survival and Broken Dreams ...125

1. Debra Gardner - The forgotten heartbeat 126
2. Mary Martin - Say a little prayer 141
3. Queen Irena - An intimate passage to new-ness 152
4. Dr Gloria N Harrison - At the end of the tunnel 164
5. Uki Asemota - Love kept me sane 178

Part Four: Abuse, Pain, Fear and Freedom 193

1. Lucy Arenberg - The journey is the destination 194
2. Blake Taylor - The parent's lottery 205
3. Penny Hollick - Behind the looking glass 215
4. Jay Jay Williams - Darkest hours 227
5. Laura Buxo - Trick or Treat 240

Conclusion 252

About the Publisher 255

Book Projects.uk 257

INTRODUCTION

"When we do the best, we can, we never know what miracle is wrought in our life, or in the life of another."

– Helen Keller

This book is about women who appear from the outside to have the perfect lives, but when you look a little further you find that is far from the truth. The journey that life has taken them is far from being straight forward and smooth. In many cases, it is full of heartache, misery and torture. Hurt can be both mental and physical. It can be delivered instantly or continuously.

If you touch a hot surface, the sudden jolt of pain pulls your hand away fast to minimise the damage caused. This is not the case if the surface is warm and the heat is turned up slowly. Before you know it, your skin is sticking to the hot surface and you cannot pull away without leaving some of yourself behind. This is like the toxic relationships in which some women have found themselves trapped. They desperately want to leave, but part of them is stuck there and they cannot pull away. The longer they wait the worse it gets, and the damage caused to them just gets worse. Eventually they accept the damage as the pain is too intense and they have no choice to pull away or they will die.

The title of this book is *Love Unboxed*. I have not mentioned the feeling of "Love" yet. Love is the passion that the twenty women that have contributed to this book have for other women. It has taken real bravery for them to open their hearts and souls to publish their "real" stories behind the make-up, broad smiles and their corporate name tags.

"Learn to enjoy every minute of your life. Be happy now. Don't wait for something outside of yourself to make you happy in the future. Think how precious is the time you should spend, whether it's at work or with your family. Every minute should be enjoyed and savored."

~ Earl Nightingale

LOVE UNBOXED: AN ANTHOLOGY BY WOMEN FOR WOMEN

PART ONE

PASSION, ROMANCE, FAIRY TALE

COURAGEOUS WOMEN
Placida Acheru: United Kingdom

"It took me quite a long time to develop a voice, and now that I have it, I am not going to be silent."

~ Madeleine Albright

I have wanted to commission a book about women for many years. Women need a voice and a platform to share their message. I believe in the collaboration of hearts and souls to help other women rise and be their best self. This is a book to say you are not alone. You have strength. I hope this book helps you find that passion inside, to find the real you and to see it bloom.

Many decisions in life are made in a split second because they seem the best choice at the time. From the stories these amazing women have shared, there is a common theme that each knew in the back of their minds that this was not the correct decision to make, yet in every case, we all walked straight in front of that speeding truck. In a few cases, the choice to walk in front of that speeding truck was a cry for help, a scream to be heard or an action to get noticed. In each case, we failed to use our intuition, our inner strength and to make the right decision and stop to let the speeding truck pass by.

It is not my intention to dwell of how difficult it is to recover from being hit by a speeding truck, but I know from my own story that it can take quite some time. I have been fortunate, and my prayers have been answered and somebody, an English man, who against all the odds grabbed me literally by the hand, pulled me back (originally against my will) and has not let go ever since.

AN ANTHOLOGY BY WOMEN FOR WOMEN

As a child and growing up, I always thought I would meet one person, get married, have kids and grow old with that one person. I was going to lead a fairy tale life of knights, castles and rose gardens. Life's plan had a different story for me. It took me on a path where the words, "I love you" started to have no meaning. When I heard the words, the substance and real meaning behind them was missing. It had reached the point that I started to feel that I was the problem. We always start to feel it is the woman's fault. It is our failure.

You might wonder why a person who is branded as a "Business Coach" is compiling a book about Love! I was motivated by my hurting deep inside. I am a Top Business Transformation Coach, Multi-Time Bestselling Author, Founder, Mentor, Digital Strategist, the list goes on. With all the business tags, I had no love in my life. I was working hard building my business, putting myself out there to attract clients, enjoying the buzz and excitement of being out there talking to people, helping, then going home alone, to an empty flat. No one to share my day with. No one to keep me warm at night. I was helping develop people. Helping them find strength, but completely neglecting myself. I had been hurt and abandoned too often to look for love anymore. It was not welcome in my life, but by giving up on it, I was in fact giving up on me. I am writing this book because I found the strength to accept love. I always will. I want to help others find it too. The best way I feel I can do that is to show you other women and prove you are not alone. It will happen if you visualise it enough and do not give up on yourself.

You will see that in each of these stories each woman had to find a love of "themselves" first. By starting to love yourself, you will find that you begin attracting love into your own life. I am not saying it is easy. You need to find the space to take a step back from the pressures you are under that are suppressing this love. And once you do, make loving yourself the priority.

I pray that you find strength within the pages of this book. Each story has its own power and will resonate differently with different people. The one that is in tune with you will be your story, your strength. It will be your redemption and the rope that will help you climb out of your predicament and find love of yourself.

The contributing authors are women from diverse races and cultures. We have done our best not to take away the uniqueness of their voice and writing. Open your mind, read, enjoy. My one request to you is, support these women by leaving a review, it would mean a lot to them. Thank you.

ADVENTURE HEALING
Christina Tindle: United States

"I have learned that if you must leave a place that you have lived in and loved and where all your yesteryears are buried deep, leave it any way except a slow way, leave it the fastest way you can. Never turn back and never believe that an hour you remember is a better hour because it is dead. Passed years seem safe ones, vanquished ones, while the future lives in a cloud, formidable from a distance. The cloud clears as you enter it. I have learned this, but like everyone, I learned it late."

~ Beryl Markum, British Aviator, 1902-1986

FLYING TO THE SUN

Many think Icarus was foolish for flying too close to the sun. Not me. He helped me realize how much higher I should go. That's why, after I learned of my husband's extensive infidelity and white-collar crimes, I decided upon a lifestyle change equally as shocking: I learned to fly. Flight instruction was a metaphor for lofty healing I sought. My heart crashed when I heard about the affairs and illegal activity that dated back before we met. Shame was tough because, as a counselor, I "should have known better." I forgave myself because a narcissistic sociopath is hard to detect even for professionals. I had fallen for fake charm and put my heart and all my money into a relationship supposed to be based on trust and lost it all. I refused to be grounded in pain and decided that flying was the perfect antidote.

The desire to fly hit like a thunderbolt and a current of electricity shot through me as if Cupid's arrow pierced my heart. A love affair with myself, a healing overhaul really, initiated. Flying distracted the misery and emotional shock. After years married to someone who never loved me, I had given away the best parts of me. I hadn't known my worth then and sliced off more of me to help the relationship work. Finally, when little was left of my heart, it disengaged. Learning to fly repaired deep pain through adventure that demanded commitment to the present. There was no way to quit or cheat during a flight and I needed something that forced me to move ahead. Flight metaphorically taught perspectives how to manage turbulence, compute center of gravity, take offs, safe landings, navigation, headwinds, and tailwind, all forces which existed in my personal life as well. The lessons were an active way to sooth betrayed trust. In order to ever love again, I couldn't remain stuck in a quagmire of humiliation and agony. I had to rise above the injustice, so I flew as high as I could go.

The lessons began with self-honesty. My truth was that I hadn't been happy with my spouse for years no matter how important saving a marriage seemed. After much conflict and lies, I eventually forgot that I deserved better. Limiting thoughts electrified neural circuits which primed my brain's chemistry for lower expectations. When I finally admitted that I was unhappy, he assured me I didn't deserve more. But in the cockpit, that lie was confronted. Negativity evaporated like magic as I operated each aircraft. Optimism visited, infrequently at first, but then became a regular co-pilot on travels. I learned to navigate airplanes and my life where I wanted to go by first admitting that where I came from was unacceptable and I deserved better.

The door to darkness opened wider over time and let in more hope. I knew that I would be okay. Mihaly Csikszentmihalyi, expert on happiness and creativity stated that, "True happiness involves the pursuit of worthy goals." He believed happiness was dependent upon, "what one does to be happy." Since my marriage lacked love, and love must be fed to survive, I transferred my passion to flying instead. Airborne adventures unfolded powerful, present moments and offered formidable opportunities that challenged self-defeating beliefs about my worth. It was the first time in a long while that I had fun doing something for myself and I delighted in the freedom from worries and anguish as I flew. Every climb after take-off taught me to raise personal expectations and reinforced a life adventure based in positive well-being.

Next, I let go of fear in order to operate an aircraft…. and my new life…solo. Fear had sabotaged decisions by guiding only towards what I thought was possible, not to what I wanted most, because it appeared safer. I had resisted divorce initially because I was afraid of change and worried that living alone might not be easy since I was in my 50's. Actor Jim Carrey once shared that his father wanted to be a stand-up comedian but didn't believe he'd make enough income to take care of his family. Instead, he took a safe job as an accountant. After 12 years, he was fired and the family struggled financially for a long time afterwards. Carrey stated, "You can fail at what you don't want so you may as well take a chance on doing what you love." That struck me. Fear had bullied by using self-defeating beliefs like I don't deserve better or I can't manage. When I admitted I also wanted to have fun, act silly, trust, and create adventures, I stopped living accidentally and started to create legendary dreams.

Gratitude was another vital practice. I became thankful that the marriage ended because I fell in love with me, my passions, and respected my boundaries. When I passed the check ride six months later, I appreciated the self-care and time I had invested. Flying demanded focus, concentration, and flight planning so there was little time to worry or feel sorry for myself. Insecurities diminished, and I discovered that my strengths were only beaten down, not permanently destroyed. I often wondered who I would have become had I taken the path of least resistance and succumbed to the destructive relationship...and stayed. The empowerment gained from piloting airplanes invigorated me and I guarded that love by not giving it away to the wrong people. Gratitude increased my resilience to endure.

Persistence was my toughest master though. Repetition was essential to ingrain pilot proficiency so if I ended a flight disappointed, that became the next flight mission to master. Just as when my heart broke from the betrayal of trust, I then expected a stronger commitment to myself. Personal growth enhanced flight lessons and continued long after the marriage ended. Flying didn't come easily but by setting goals, I persisted. Even five years later I advanced into backcountry instruction as a bush pilot flying taildraggers just to push proficiency even higher.

WOMAN GONE WILD

Idaho bush pilots flew mountainous terrain, descended into canyons, soared over rivers, and crossed meadows from above. It was the ultimate flight precision I figured, and that dedication to skill encouraged me onward. Backcountry aviation combined flights with hiking, backpacking, or fishing, passions that I stopped during the marriage since my ex didn't like them. To be a bush pilot in Idaho meant I had to overcome inner demons that said I couldn't and emotional limits that warned I shouldn't. Wilderness flying became the next tier closer to my sun and it took two years of persistent practice to fly the six million acres of this magical recreational playground proficiently.

At first, I was intimidated. The Frank Church River of No Return Wilderness, or simply called "The Frank" by locals, is the largest forested wilderness in the lower 48 states. Few places in America, and nowhere else besides Alaska, provide a wilderness that compliments the magnitude of The Frank. It's a land of deep canyons and rugged mountains where white water rivers define boundaries. The main Salmon River runs westward along the north boundary. The Middle Fork of the Salmon, my favorite area, flows from the southern boundary northward for 100 miles with 100 rapids, until it joins the Main Salmon. Forests of Douglas fir and Lodgepole pine thrived and were divided by grassy meadows or sun-washed, treeless slopes. The rugged area provided habitat for a wide variety of birds and mammals including a large population of mountain lions and grey wolves. Communities of black bears, as well as lynx, red fox, and coyote scattered throughout. Bighorn sheep, mountain goats, moose, elk, mule deer, and white tail deer flourished. It was easy to get lost, to overrun short airstrips, or get caught in canyon weather. It was where I expanded personal limitations, inside and out, and carved a new romantic life.

Art-appreciation anchored my personal growth journey when I recalled what Elrey Jeppesen, an American aviation pioneer who created navigation charts, once said, "There is a big difference between a pilot and an aviator. One is a technician; the other is an artist in love with flight." It clicked for me how planes were an aerial paintbrush flown over airy canvases with a commitment to technique, the sort that joins colorful joy with moment of truths. From above, I enhanced nature's portrait by strokes of sun angle, shading, and glamorous earth tones.

The Frank taught me how to release a bigger part of

myself that had never existed. As I flew the daunting terrain, inner dialogues opened that had been blocked by hectic schedules, failed love, and narrow thinking. I had buried my joy beneath a sad marriage and the silent screams that urged me to escape went unheard. But as I navigated the grand wilderness of central Idaho, I simultaneously listened to a deeper wilderness within and learned I mattered...to me. It didn't make a difference anymore that my marriage failed. Sometimes I could almost see my heart flying outside my airplane with a grin matching mine. My heart, mind, and soul synchronized and I felt giddy with love, only this time, not for a man who repeatedly betrayed me. Flying fed my wounded self-esteem many soul-nourishing meals until eventually my heart smiled again. I appreciated who I had become and compared my personal improvement against each flight's progress until inner scales tipped over to positivity...for good.

When the backcountry training concluded, my Best Self appeared.

DEVELOPING A DEEPER BOND

The crux of life, I realized, was to give back the best part of me to others. So, to share my passion of flying and the wilderness, I invited my brother to the Middle Fork of the Salmon River to camp for a few days for his birthday. This invitation validated confidence in my flight skills and reinforced a commitment for an adventurous lifestyle.

A deeper bond developed between my brother and I as we fished and talked over campfires. After the trip, he snapped a telling photo of me as I leaned against 31" Tundra Tires of my taildragger airplane. Inner peace radiated out through my smile. He caught an instant more notable than one would have guessed. Confidence smiled back broadly in that picture. Full appreciation for how high I had come since my worst days hit me. Never could I have imagined me so happy, strong, or competent back then. Flying reclaimed parts of me that had atrophied from pain and humiliation. Aerial adventures inspired self-awareness instead of pity with each nautical mile aloft. When the shutter closed on that picture, it was obvious that I would never have flown my brother into Idaho's wilderness had I remained who I was in that marriage. Instead, I was free, alive, and becoming a better person. Adventure linked confidence to self-esteem and then returned my heart to its rightful owner...me.

When the grief faded, joyful moments exploded into poetic beauty more often. Flying became my action art that displayed priceless views witnessed by few. This artistic expression was in concert with science and math, balanced by personal challenge, and enlivened a spirited personality. It also removed choking comfort zones and amplified choices instead. Operating a buoyant cockpit above the land,

LOVE UNBOXED

I escaped noise and frantic-manic-panics about nothing truly important and merged into the lovely wild: clouds, wind, sun, abeam granite peaks, above elegant animals, beneath blue sky. Flight honed competence, and because I persisted, confidence flourished from an appreciation of living a full life. Aviation adventure opened a direct channel to my heart, poured an elixir of grace and healing self-worth that intensified fresh insight, as it charged my fun meter. A positive feedback loop of happiness resulted and it red-lined on each adventure. I learned to laugh at myself, at life, and with others. The pain finally suffocated and deserted its post.

Anytime I look at the photo my brother took of me on that trip, I am reminded of cherished images that etched into my mind. Those experiences altered the essence of who I was, reshaped by flying Idaho's wilderness. Endless aviation Kodak moments developed over the years in the dark room of my healing heart. Like the time when a wolf loped across Cold Meadows airstrip as I rolled out on landing, or negotiated rough gopher holes at Chamberlain Basin to avoid getting stuck. I enjoyed tummy-grinning uplifts from sunny ridges, and have been mesmerized by white rapids below on the Selway River. Another time I banked hard to out-climb a flock of snow geese after take-off. On one flight, my visibility was obscured when a fog of bugs splattered the entire windshield while birds twisted in a feeding frenzy overhead. And once when reunited with my taildragger after a multi-day hike, over 200 horseflies were ousted that took up residence in the wing struts. I have departed the 1600' Solider Bar airstrip into thin air over a 500' drop to the river and can still see details in my mind in the opposing rock wall as it loomed closer. I ferried my daughter to a backcountry camp, the only woman to fly-in her child. Surrounding father-pilots watched as I hefted my daughter's bags onto the 4-wheeler. Finally, one asked which charter I flew for as the others listened attentively. I teased, "Women-Gone-Wild," and got a chuckle from my ten-year old daughter. Accessible only by plane, I've flown to remote trail heads and discovered happy places hidden deep within me. From my first landing in the wilderness, astonished when on final seeing mountain goats balanced on craggy peaks, backcountry flying became my life purpose. And that purpose was about loving myself. I learned from painting romantic adventures aloft on my own aviation canvases that I AM, and I CAN… love myself, love others, and improve.

Thanks to my pilot's license, today I am a lover of soul-expanding flights because adventure reboots the ordinary with magic. I could not be what I wanted to be by remaining who I was. I chose a healing adventure instead. With every engine start, feet come alive, RPMs accelerate, flaps retract, and as land drops away, another aeronautical oilcloth awaits extraordinary composition. As an aviator-artist, I committed to a kaleidoscopic life adventure. In those views, I left my heart and returned to rejuvenate. I'm grateful for the legend of Icarus that showed me to fly higher than I first dared. Once untethered from limited, negative thinking and lifeless love, I soared even higher. The sky was my only limit and flight revived a life of inner romance.

ABOUT THE AUTHOR

Christina is a Licensed Professional Counselor and Personal Transformation Coach with a Master's degree in Psychology. She re-frames personal challenges into positive growth activating individual strengths and passions that build direction, momentum, happiness, leadership, creativity, health, wealth, & peak performance. She guides clients to higher satisfaction and believes when people answer the call of passion, deeper joy and confidence result. Her uplifting evidence-based approach to change is based in positive psychology, cognitive-bias training, Buddhist philosophy, excellent communication skills, transformational humor, and compassion. Christina lives her truth. She earned a pilot's license 25 years ago and flies Idaho's wilderness in her taildragger. She raced vintage race cars several years and regularly competes in the 20-mile Boulder Mountain skate ski race. Regardless of outcomes, adventures demand commitment to living fully, a notion that Christina embraces completely.

CONTACT

Website: www.christinatindle.com
Email: backcountryflygirl@gmail.com

WHEN ALL HOPE IS LOST
Chantal Edie N: Cameroon

"My love was unleashed where I least expected; I had lost all hope of ever finding love. When I had resigned that due to my 'fatness' and introversion men weren't interested in me. "

I WASN'T CREATED TO BE HAPPY

No way! It's not meant for me; "I wasn't created to be happy", I thought to myself. It was like a magical thing to see two amorous people walking hands locked in. I had lost all trust in man and its humanity. "Don't worry guys, I will tell you how this happened."

In 2007 before travelling to England to further my studies, I had had a five-year long relation with a guy I had met on my first year in University. I was 22 and he was 27; He was handsome and intelligent but very poor and quick to anger. I loved him and was his provider; I never minded. I would always steal food from my auntie's house and I remember the day I was nearly caught in the act; I nearly died of fear. We appeared much loved up and my friends were quite envious of me for landing such a cutie. I remember the day he slapped me" Domi you slapped me", I latched out with tears flowing down my cheeks. We had been together then for three years and the angel transformed into a demon before my eyes. I know you are wondering what could have caused this brutal action. Well, nothing bad that I did; he just became jealous when I smiled with his friends, if a random guy yelled out "hey baby, your beautiful" This particular day, everyone at home thought I had gone for classes but in reality, I hadn't a class on that day and as usual I was at his place instead. It was a single room in a very remote neighborhood and we had only his tiny bed and an electric heater. I had brought some food to cook; to be more précised rice and tomato. There was one thing lacking and that was meat; so Domi headed up the road and got some meat for 500 frs to add flavor to the food. He did not have a TV set, so we spent our time talking and playing.

It was 5:00 pm when he went to see me to the roadside. We were going through a lane where most of the bad boys in the neighborhood sat to smoke and chat over how the government had let them down when suddenly one of the boys called yelled out in French "bebe tu est belle!" And some other obscenities. I saw fire in domis eyes, he suddenly became red with anger and spat back at the guy; "you bloody idiot, she is not your match" and you know there is no better way of starting a fight in the hood, right?

The guy quickly got on his feet as if he has been waiting for this opportunity all his life; the two started spitting promises of death to each other's face. I had to do something; I short as I was 1.54m stepped in between 2 angry giants; pushed the guy who wasn't my boyfriend away at the same time praying to God to intervene. I was so scared he was going to beat my boyfriend blue and black; guy looked like he has been lifting weights all his life! Thank God, I the guy seemed to like me enough to heed to my demand that he leaves us alone. I was banned from ever taking that road ever, even though it was the shortest way to my house and was called a whore because I had a short skirt on. He just had to put the blame on me and the blame continued the next day at the campus; reproaching me of smiling and acting too cool with his friends.

I was baptized with a new name "l'allumeusse "; the seductive. As time went on I was made to feel I was ugly and even called dirty; We had morning classes on that day when I saw him across the am phi theatre, naturally I left my friends to go and greet him and to my very surprise I was received with a "your so dirty, what the hell is this?!" I was bewildered and looked at myself repeatedly trying to find out what was wrong. Then he pointed with so much disdain in his voice, "Look at your neck, it's disgusting!" I touched it and realized that the skin around my neck had peeled off as a result of the face mask I had applied last night. I was so shocked and embarrassed tears filled my eyes and I mumbled "I am sorry".

Later on, in the day I brought up the subject and told him I hated the way he reproached me in public and that if it continues I would leave him one of these days. From there a quarrel sparked off and he gave me the slap of my life. Time stood still and as I glared at him. "Domi you dared slap me", I latched out with tears flowing down my cheeks. I stood up wore my shoes and left, and I swore to myself that that was it! As usual he came to my house pleaded and I took him back. My liberation came when I left to study in England and how easy it was to forget him.

My cousin caught a money transfer I had done to him after only one week in England and reported to my uncle who preached and put some sense in my head, then I realised I am not his provider, love has no price, this isn't love.

LOVE IS DECEITFUL

My love chapter in England wasn't any rosy; News had spread like wild fire about my arrival in the Cameroonian community and I almost thought I was the prettiest girl in town until I was awoken! Upon my arrival I was received into my cousin's home and just two weeks there I got a job at the burger king, the first week there and body ached like I had moored a hectare of land, seriously! That day I couldn't anymore, my waist and feet were killing me, so I took off although my manager wasn't impressed at all "look" she said in her very polish accent "you must be strong to work here!"

Well I got home and slept for what seemed like forever; only 2 hrs. actually. I was called downstairs and my cousin's husband handed the phone to me. At the other end was this guy with a peculiar accent| [a mixture of Bakossi and English], he heard I was here and wanted to say hi and a lot of bla bla[at that time I did not consider it blab la blab I must confess] He continued calling and making me feel wanted and god knows I needed that at that time or so I thought. That was the beginning of my love struggle in Basingstoke.

We had this general meeting and he came down from the north and after talking every day on the phone for over a month we met finally. He was handsome and well-built although he was over doing the confidence thing, but I thought I had found my prince charming. Well, it only took a day to understand that I was living in dream land. We were sited on the stairs while the party was going on. He presented me to his sister who hugged me affectionately and then bluntly told me "don't let him fool you, he is married already" and I thought she was joking but nope she wasn't. I couldn't believe it, I cried more from being fooled and led along especially as he had desperately wanted to have sex with me the night before, the very day we met.

If you are 38 and chasing pussy like a rabid dog, it might be time to put a leash on it and contemplate your end game. My cousin's husband couldn't understand my pain and thought I was "hungry for a man "being a typical chauvinist that he was. Eventually he was going back home to marry his fiancée, but ass hole kept trying to convince me of his love for me, "if only I had met you two months before" he squirmed

It did not last long before I was consoled by another

man; affectionate and caring. We moved in together and lived together for two years. My uncles never appreciated that I was "in a relationship with some guy who "did not have papers" but I had no care in the world. I thought I was in love and happy. Finally, it was found out he wasn't clean and we both decided he went back home. He became my responsibility and I did everything to make him happy by providing money for him to invest in his business. I remember the day I understood that it was all a wasteful relationship. I was living as a live-in carer, taking care of an elderly couple and I had my room upstairs, so I had to run down the stairs every time the needed my attention. That day I was on a skype call with him when suddenly the buzzer rang, and I dashed downstairs, leaving him on skype. I stayed about 30 mins and upon my return to skype with him I saw a very young girl standing hands wrapped around his neck and I heard him promising to give her money as soon as he can. That was a shocker and I screamed his name and said, "what are you doing?" and his reply was pathetic denial that what I saw wasn't really. Only then did I realise that I had fallen out of love with him already because I wasn't hurt in my heart, only felt bad knowing I was the one providing him all his financial needs.

HOW I MET MY SON'S FATHER

I have had this long Facebook relationship forever, he was there to console me and even till today he is still there for me. We became friends in 2010 on Facebook and we did discuss hours on end about all and sundry. He was there for me when I lost my sister, when I had a hard time renewing my papers and he encouraged, prayed with me. In sept 2011 His brother came to England to study and just after two weeks in London, he rushed down Southampton to see me. He was younger than me, very handsome and cunning. He never wanted me to tell his brother he visited even though I insisted we do. He had his plans and which he had started planting even before we met.

He knew I was lonely and depressed; I still hadn't digested the death of my only sister and I was going through a lot renewing my student visa. He was so bold and gave me a lot of his time and attention; I knew I wasn't in love with him, but I was just so happy to have him around me. Then I received a letter letting me know my student visa was not renewed and I was in such a pitiful state. Steve had just been in the country for five months and he couldn't bare the stress and his mask fell off. He became angry and distant, he came to see me for the last time a week before I left for my country and I discovered a month later that he had left me pregnant.

LOVE IN CAMEROON

My love was unleashed where I least expected; I had lost all hope of ever finding love. When I had resigned that due to my 'fatness' and introversion men weren't interested in me. I had a hard time accepting that my son was not recognized by his father until now. He has a father now in my fiancée. I know you're curious to know how we met, I and my Zacharie; our passion for PHOTOGRAPHY brought us together. I was invited by a fashion designer as a fashion critic while Zach was the photographer for the event.

When I saw him, I went to him to help him with his bags of equipment and we engaged in a conversation. I had never heard of him before even though he was the one doing the billboards for the top agencies in Douala, Cameroon. After the event I assist him with his bags and coincidentally his studio was just near my office. At that time, I was working in a maritime company and was just a few days from leaving the job to partner in business as a marketing director for another maritime company. Zach's eyes lit when he heard I have been into photography since 2010; we were in 2015 and I was so excited to show him all my photographic works. He had only good things to say about my work and that made me so happy.

The day after I had two tickets to Stromaes concert {an international artist from France] and thank God Zach liked his music because he left all his engagements and went with me to the concert. Very naturally we held hands, dances and screamed to the music, it was such a fun night. We trekked all the way back and even though I had platform shoes on I did not feel any discomfort walking hand in hand with him and nothing else really mattered around us. He took me to eat and after to a club; did we even dance? But I still remember the longest kiss experience; he just touched my face and kissed me. We started working together and in 2016 I officially became his business partner as we moved into our new studio. I was 34 years old when I found and kept love. We have gone through the most difficult time together, a time when my heart froze and yearned for the underworld. One day I shall gather the strength to narrate the 'unimaginable'.

THE WEDDING PROPOSAL

On the 18th of May I woke up happy and wore a black dress, I had my nails done a day before, flip flops on my feet and heels in my hand. I was going out for a dinner date with my girls. In the office Zach was the first to remind me it was time for me to go and he kindly dropped me at my friend's place. I was greeted with a rose flower from Doreen and it immediately brought tears to my eyes; memories of my baby made my heart faint and I just had to sit down.

Doreen told me she was given the rose in church and even when Adeline handed me another rose, I immediately thought she also got it from church. I was thinking to myself "I will drop these on her grave" a painful ritual which hurt but brought me closer to her. We entered the restaurant, it was new and cosy, no one insight but the waitress. I was wondering where Beryl was when Doreen stepped out pretending to call her. I panicked when I saw Zach's friends come in with cameras and roses.

Everyone was handing roses to me, then it hit me; Zach planned this all! I looked over my shoulder towards the door and saw him walk in panting, he went on his knees and asked me to marry him, with tears flowing down my cheeks I kissed him and said, "yes my love" He proposed on the 18th of May, it was a surprise proposal and my friends got me really good.

Now we are planning our wedding for next year. Even though the saying goes that "there's no perfect relationship" I am happy where I am with Zach, I thought him how to love just the way I wanted to be loved. Sometimes I am low other times I am happy but what's certain is" I am happy where I am."

ABOUT THE AUTHOR

Chantal Edie was born in 1981 in Bangem, Cameroon. She has a masters 1 in political sciences, a Bachelors in History from the University of Yaounde in Cameroon and an HND in health and social care from the Impact international college in Reading. She is not a conventional person and believes that she can do anything she sets her mind too. No wonder she became an operations manager for a maritime company in Douala. She is currently a maritime consultant and co-owner of Studioxldouala one of the most prestigious studios in Cameroon. Her passion for photography sprang from the views she saw during her walks in a small village in Southampton, Bursledon. Chantal was a part of the Media workshop in Southampton where she developed photographic skills as seen in the work she produces. She is also a blogger and the founder of African woman in photography an online platform showcasing the work of African female photographer

CONTACT

Website: https://www.studioxldouala.com/
Email: c.edie@studioxldouala.com

TAKING CHANCES
Ify Ojo: Canada

"Pay attention to the things you are naturally drawn to. They are often connected to your path, passion, and purpose in life. Have the courage to follow them."

~ Ruben Chavez

A WAKE-UP CALL

The plane touched down at the Vancouver International Airport and I was glad to be back to home in British Columbia, to the loving embrace of my family, after a hectic week in London for Africa Fashion Week London (AFWL).

A simple email to a virtual stranger, a London based award-winning fashion designer led to the sponsorship of her collection at the AFWL which culminated with my visit to the UK.

Just a year earlier my husband had received a job offer that necessitated our move from Winnipeg Manitoba, a place we called home for 17 years, to the beautiful western province of British Columbia.

We loaded all our worldly goods into a moving truck that left a day earlier then hit the road for the 24-hour ride between the two provinces.

As the wheat fields of the prairies gradually faded behind us, the welcoming outlines of the jagged mountains in Calgary Alberta came into view. Tired and exhausted, we exited the highway to the closest decent hotel we could find. The next day, we drove onward, navigating the winding, sometimes treacherous, roads that opened up to the awe inspiring, drop-down-on-your-knees-now views of glacier-fed lakes and the majestic snow-capped mountains of the Canadian Rockies. They looked like natural cathedrals, hewn by the elements over millennia, bearing testament to the greatness of the loving hand of our Creator.

My trepidation mounted as we drove closer and closer to our final destination.

I had placed some trust in my husband's judgment, by agreeing that he could go ahead and purchase our new home although my only impressions of the house were gleaned from pictures from a real estate website. There was simply no time to fly to British Columbia to inspect the house with him. We decided it was best to purchase it immediately since the opportunity to do so became available, because stalling for as little as a few weeks would mean being priced out of our budget due to the competitive nature of purchasing real estate in BC.

We pulled up the driveway in pitch darkness and walked into our new home. A quick inspection quickly allayed my fears. My good man, I thought. He had made a great choice. Morning welcomed us with a stunning view of Ombré Mountains. Silently I prayed that I'd never be blind to its ever-unfolding beauty.

The following weeks were filled with the brisk activity of unpacking, decorating, settling the kids into school and learning the lay of the land. I quickly settled into the familiar routine of job searching when normalcy finally returned to our lives. However, during that time, a listlessness and fear dogged my efforts. I shrugged this off on several occasions and I trudged on, sending off resumes to different companies. But one evening, during a mindless scan of Instagram posts, I came across a quote by Maya Mendoza that stopped me in my tracks.

> *"No amount of security is worth the suffering of a mediocre life chained to a routine that has killed your dreams."*

Those words echoed and gave voice to all my longings of breaking free from the rigid 9-5 schedule. Memories of the cold winter mornings when I'd wake up and drag myself off the bed flooded my mind. Heedlessly, I'd get in and out of the shower, slap on a little paint and powder, then head off to work. I would go about my routine like a machine on auto pilot. Smile, nod, doodle through a meeting. *I was dying on the inside!*

Many times, I would wonder, is this it? But why was I was walking back willingly to my jailer? What had I traded my dreams for? A steady pay check, six-week paid vacation earned after five years of employment, an employee company stock ownership? But was it worth doing this again? I laughed because I knew the answer.

Funny thing about change: it forces you out of an inertia created by familiar and comfortable routines that come with the normalcy surrounding our lives. Just a few months ago when I was still blindly zoned into the routine in Winnipeg, coming across Maya Mendoza's quote would have had little or no affect. Just like that, everything was suddenly different.

So here I was, at midlife. I started drawing again, drawing faces with features and colours similar to mine and all the while my dreams fermented. But why was I drawing those faces? I guess it was an unconscious desire to make up for the lack of diversity in the area of British Columbia we had moved to. I chuckled because it reminded me of the time when my then 3-year-old son, Michael, tapped me on my legs and inquired with great seriousness if the African drummers in a painting I had just completed were his uncles.

Being naturally gifted as an artist, I considered several entrepreneurial directions. But my love for fabrics and textiles, which was passed on by my mother and grandmother, finally made my decision to transition to textile design an easy one. Those faces I had drawn naturally converted to patterns that I printed on my first fabric designs.

Musings about change and taking chances brought memories of my younger self to mind. She was someone I'd almost forgotten with the passage of time. Long before cynicism borne out of experiences turned her into a cautious adult who looked twice before leaping. Many years before, she had taken a direction in her life that was based on the promptings of her finer perceptions, and that led to her love story; a story that started with very humble beginnings.

THE MEETING

"Intuition is a spiritual faculty and does not explain, but simply points the way."

Florence Scovel Shinn

Sweat trickled down my spine and I squirmed uncomfortably as I stood hand in hand in Immanuel Fellowship Church with my soon-to-be husband in a hot and languid summer day in Winnipeg, Manitoba. The simmering humidity made the simple $50 dress I had converted into a wedding gown cling to me like a second skin. I was surprised at the comfort of my cheap beige Walmart pumps; it was the only thing that stopped me from running out of the church and tearing the uncomfortable dress off. My handsome groom stood tall, looking oblivious to the heat, in a navy-blue blazer that was still in decent shape, though he had worn it so many times before.

There we were, after years of dating, taking our vows with Pastor Deborah officiating. Ours was a simple $300 budget wedding. That's all we had and all we could afford. We had both resolved not to bother our parents who lived far away in Nigeria for anything. My hair and make-up were done free by "Aunty" Grace, a hairdresser friend of ours. Bouquet was donated by my kindly "Aunty" Bernice, food and entertainment in the church basement was donated by the warm-hearted members of the church, and my newly minted brother-in-law, "Uncle" G, was the official photographer for the day.

I smiled as I remembered our first date, which was a few weeks after meeting briefly through a mutual friend. My friend had mentioned in her off hand and playful manner that the guy who had given us a ride from a party really, really liked me. I squinted, trying to remember who he was, and then I remembered. I had caught him stealing glances at me more than a few times through the rear-view mirror as he navigated the dusty streets of Ibadan that night.

He giggled nervously like a teen when we were finally introduced at our second meeting. That totally turned me off. I cringed, simultaneously recoiling mentally in revulsion when he took my hand and shook it with palms dripping with sweat – but inwardly embracing him in spirit, feeling a shift like a home coming. There was a familiarity and ease with him, which felt like coming face to face with a long-lost love.

We bonded over his expertise in Nigerian jollof rice. He loved cooking it, I loved eating it. There was no wooing, no courtship; for some strange reason neither of us questioned there was no labelling in our relationship. It began as a friendship that we both left to evolve naturally from one stage to another.

A few of my friends were surprised at this new relationship. Hmm, he's not even in the "*happening*" crowd, he's not even "*toosh*", you guys are not on the same level *oo*, abeg, what do you see in him? One commented, waving his hand from the top of my head to my feet, "Look at you, *lepa*, fine girl! You don't even know your "market value"." Shuddering, I asked if I was a piece of merchandise hung out in a stall for the highest bidder. "What value can you give to pure and unadulterated love?" I asked. He threw back his head and laughed derisively.

We parted ways. I knew whoever married him in the future would be one lucky girl, but circumstances at that time led me to believe it wouldn't be me.

A NEW EXPERIENCE

"Everything you want lies on the other side of learning to trust yourself. Take a chance. Have faith. You already know who you are, what you want, and where you want to go." Vironika Tugaleva

We reconnected years later while I was in the US and he in Canada, and our families in Nigeria finally met for formal introductions. The introduction went smoothly by all accounts, but it still drew a few hisses from some relatives from my side of the family. They pointed out that I would be the fourth of five sisters to be married to a man not belonging the Igbo tribe, an ethnic group native to the southeastern part of Nigeria. Hia! They exclaimed, and would start to talk, speculating that we are Osu! The Osu is a caste of people in Igboland with whom social interaction and marriage were discouraged because ancient laws and practices deemed them to be slaves and untouchables. Marrying people from other tribes was often their only recourse.

My husband-to-be was Yoruba, an ethnic group primarily from the southwestern side of Nigeria. Both tribes have a healthy and mutual distrust for one another. The Igbos regard the Joie de vivre of the Yoruba, which is a sharp contrast to their business oriented nature, with and an air of inferiority and suspicion. These people will spend their last kobo just to party! Even if they don't have money they will borrow just to be seen in fine lace!

Also, Yoruba men, in general, are thought by the Igbos to be inclined to polygamy, having several wives and concubines. Hmm, the way these people see marriage is not the way we see it oo, another Yoruba man Kwa?

Unfortunately, this my Yoruba man had some extra baggage as well. "We heard he lives in a pastor's basement in Canada. He doesn't have a job, they'll both starve!"

"ọbụrụ na ị na ilo awo, lo nke nwere àkwá!" àkwá!" If you are going to swallow a frog, you may as well swallow the one with eggs. If one was bent on doing something that was to be frowned upon, better be sure it was something with some benefit that was obvious to everyone, they said. See my Wahala! I was told my gentleman father finally silenced everyone when he said in his characteristic eloquence and wisdom, "Ify has proven herself to be prudent and wise in so many ways and I'm sure her decision to marry this boy will not be an exception."

We forged on. I knew finding a school in Canada would be the fastest way to be with him. I found one within a few months of searching and got accepted. School started soon after.

Winnipeg winter showed its full might that year; the -45°C wind chill made my face feel like it would freeze and fall into to a million pieces. My rude awakening came when I realised the layers of winter wear I'd piled on didn't stop the bone chilling cold, it just prevented me from dying from it. Studying interactive multimedia media and web design was a dream come true, but I was in school on a wing and prayer. We had just enough money to pay for my school fees for the first few months and no idea in the world where the rest of the money would come from.

Growing up, my mother would draw wisdom gleaned from in the light of Truth: The Grail Message in every circumstance. She'd often say that if you did anything out of love that was unselfish it would induce the laws that are anchored in our Creator's ever watchful love to conspire in your favour. This would prove to be true.

One day out of the clear blue sky, a phone call came from the lovely Ms Nicole Smith, a Chicago based art gallery owner. She informed me in her warm manner of speaking that one of my artworks on display in her gallery had been sold.

Miracle after miracle unfolded after that first call because suddenly there was brisk interest in my paintings. My paintings! Like clockwork, the checks became consistent from month to month. At the end she sold just the amount of art work I needed to pay my school fees over that period.

We finally moved out of Pastor Deborah's basement to our place, never forgetting the help and guidance she provided through those rough times.

Our little apartment didn't look shabby at all because all the garage sale treasures we had carefully scored from the wealthy neighbourhoods over the previous months found their pride of place in our new space.

Slowly and surely everything fell into place.

Our son was born the following year. I held him in my arms with this verse rising in my soul: *I will lift up mine eyes to the hills. From whence cometh my help.*

CONCLUSION

My story is not an uncommon one and I'm glad to have been given a platform to share it.

My experience has taught me to trust love and above all trust the intuition that prompts you to stay or flee in any situation. Never underestimate the power of humble beginnings it's often the foundation for harmony that may be difficult to achieve if only one person came into a relationship with all the material benefits. I looked beyond our circumstance at that time because what was most important to me was he had the inherent qualities to navigate through them.

ABOUT THE AUTHOR

Ify Ojo is the owner and principal designer of Greater Vancouver based Stela Textile Design Studio, www.stelatextiledesignstudio.com. Her love for textiles, which was passed on by her mother, Stella, has led her to textile design after more than 14 years in the web and graphic design industry.

Born and raised in Lagos, her passion is to bring a fresh and modern perspective to the African tradition of storytelling by using fabrics.

Her print designs also challenge you to look at the old with new eyes, juxtaposing ancient symbols with modern day objects.

More importantly, they tell stories that are drawn from the shared experiences of women - stories that honour, encourage and celebrate them.

She has worked with numerous designers in the fashion industry to create exclusive prints for their collections.

Ify Ojo is also co-owner of *Bibi Invitations*, an African themed wedding stationery and invitation company.

She currently resides in British Columbia and is happily married with two wonderful kids. Ollie bọbọ, a delightful Chihuahua Yorkie mix, is a recent addition to her family.

CONTACT

Website: www.ifyojo.com
Email: Ifyojo@gmail.com

PRINCE OR FROG
Gema Ramírez: Spain

"Only when the Heart is fully open, can JOY be felt and remembered. In order to move into the New World, Heaven on Earth, it is your Heart that must lead the way."

~ Isis Livingstone

MEETING THE DEADLINE

Words were not coming. The deadline to submit the draft of my story for Love Unboxed was due, I knew what I wanted to write, yet the right words were not coming to my fingers and nothing was getting typed on the blank Word document that was staring at me waiting to be filled with passion and drama.

I gave myself the Christmas period to write it. I was at home in Spain, relaxed, nothing else to do but that writing... yet Nothing...

As stress was beginning to make an appearance, in spite of the meditations I did to inspire me, I received a very unexpected WhatsApp message. Somehow, he still had my number, he managed to bypass all the blocks I put on him on and he wrote to me, on Christmas night.

After the initial shock, I decided to reply to him. I had not seen him in almost three years. He had tried to get in touch and I always blocked him or didn´t reply. I didn´t want to be dragged into his drama again, I knew the story far too well. After a conversation, he always knew how to turn things around and without realising it, we would be back together again. That is why the day I decided it was the end, I cut all possible contact.

Tonight, was different. I wanted to know what he

had to say. On Christmas night, this was sad... I was probably the only person he had available for a chat. My motherly instincts kicked in and I replied to him.

He started talking as if we had just seen each other. He had been seeing someone else for a year now, but they had split up. So, he was alone, on Christmas night and he thought of me... how kind... I knew what might have happened: they had a row and he left her... he could not handle arguments, he didn´t know any other way to react to them, he always felt unloved and finished the relationship. So, this is what happened with this new woman. I could see it so clearly, but at the same time, I knew he would come back to her in a day or two.

Something I was not expecting happened, he said: "Look, you have always been the one. I´ve been with this woman for a year and still 70% of my heart belongs to you" – I froze, but instead of melting into warmth, I broke into the more irreverent laughter when I read the next message: "So, if you come back to me now, you can still have me. Otherwise, I give you five months and I will give all my heart to this new woman". Unbelievable... I was at home, enjoying my family time, happy with my new found single status, enjoying life to its fullest. The last thing on my mind was to return to him and without knowing how, I was at the crossroads again, of returning to this man who was so willing to take me still back and give me back the whole of his rotten heart. I was moved... not... the only movement I could feel was that from my belly reacting to my laughter.

After a second or two of careful consideration, I asked, "so will you come to Spain?", I was intrigued to see how he would answer. I was so hoping to keep the comedy going, it promised to be a hilarious Christmas after all. "No", he wrote, "I live in England, I work here, you come here."

Yes, my love, I leave everything behind and come running to you, even if I have not seen you in two and a half years and you have another woman who, by the time I arrive there, would be on your bed again. What kind of selfish sick mind was that? And I was madly in love with this guy? I could not believe I had wasted seven years of my life on this relationship.

So again, carefully considering my reply, always looking out for the other person, as I am a kind and generous individual, I wrote to him, "Look... you've been with this woman for over a year now, obviously she loves you if she is still with you." (because honestly, you are such an idiot that there is no other way) "so why don´t you give this new relationship a chance and go back to her... I haven´t seen you in a long time and I will never, ever get back with you...". A long pause and then he said "Yes, you are right... you are such a nice lady, there is no-one like you... I never deserved you" blah blah blah, he continued rattling on... actually, it was nice to read those nice things about myself, but at the same time I didn't believe a word.

So, the conversation ended. I told him that he would probably end up blocking me when the woman came. He promised and re-promised that he wouldn't this time, which he wanted to keep me as friend at least... but he didn't. He blocked me again.

Mixed emotions came up. He removed hidden memories and without any notice. This new piece of information added a new level of closure to our relationship. He was living her life, enjoying a new person. I, on the other hand, had decided that I wanted to heal all of my heart before I was ready for someone new. When I was healed, I had become someone so picky that nobody was good enough to give them a chance. Maybe it was time to change... maybe I should open up and let love in again?

I wasn't sure... but one thing I knew, I had the inspiration to write now. I opened up the laptop and the words came up in a flowing river of inspiration, wit, passion and wisdom. My love story for the first volume of Love Unboxed was being born.

RECOGNISING THE ABUSER

I had gone on a date after two years of splitting up. This man was so persistent on Facebook, it was Summer... I gave him a chance. We went out for dinner. It was ok. We had conversation going, somehow there was something I could not put my finger on it, but there was something that didn´t resonate with me. He paid for dinner, even though I insisted on paying my half. We went out again the next day. We had coffee by the beach in the afternoon and then it happened... it was just one word, one single expression, the way he said it... I knew then... I knew he was the same type of guy, the abusive kind.

I left for England the next day. After the flight, on my train home, he sent me a few pictures of him and asked me to choose one for his Facebook page. "They are all good" – I said- "any of them would do, they are all so similar". "Choose one I said" – I started to shake... through his message, I could sense the energy. The energy of the abuser hidden behind niceness. Now I could spot them so easily. So, I told him, I told him I would never see him again, I explained why, he needed to know how to speak and treat a woman and he had to wise up. I told him I didn´t want anything with any man and that ultimately, I would not enter into another abusive relationship.

I knew that, if my instincts were right, I would have all sorts of verbal abuse from him on social media. I couldn´t block him on Facebook because I didn't have Facebook on my old phone. As soon as I got home, I checked. Indeed, he had sent all kinds of messages asking me to give him his money back for the dinner we shared, and he put abusive messages on my Facebook Wall.

The traits of the abuser are easy to spot:

- They are charming, and they use their charm to conquer you very quickly

  - If you start dating them, they soon tell you they love you and want to start something together really quick, like living together, build a house, get married... they don´t give you time to think and as you are in limbo all loved up by the magician in them, you say yes to all of it

  - They use little insults or words to put you down in an affectionate way first... this turns nasty after a while

  - The obvious, that sometimes we dismiss, because we want to be nice and inclusive: drug or alcohol abuse, criminal history, untreated mental illness, lack of coping mechanisms for pressure or even with other people

  - They lack self-esteem, they abuse themselves in their heads, so they end up abusing others

And abuse is not only physical abuse. Any form of violence must not be tolerated, such as:

- They call you names or put you down, disempower you
- They shout and curse
- They threaten you
- They throw things around

Get out as fast as you can. You can help them, seek help for them, but you don´t have to get involved with them, and even more, you don´t have to tolerate this type of behaviour. None of it. Tell them to look for help but don´t be their punch bag.

Practice self-love and increase your self-esteem so that you won´t attract this type of profile man anymore and you won´t fall for their charms.

The lesson was learnt for me. Now I know how to spot them and avoid more pain. But obviously, I was still attracting this type of man. I was not ready to start dating. I had to do more inner work and clean the abuser inside of me. So, I did. I kept learning and practising self-love. I concentrated my life on my new business and projects. Since Love Unboxed Book One, I have developed my niche, my brands, my coaching business.

Recently, I have come up with the workshop series UNBOX YOU, where I support people to heal their

Spiritual Hearts, incorporating meditation into their daily routines, helping them finding their life´s and soul´s purpose, changing the scarcity mindset into the mindset of Prosperity and Abundance and finally helping them develop the Conscious Leadership skills necessary to go out into the world and live the life of your dreams.

I have also created with a colleague WOMAN 5.0, where we empower women to become their best version and I have the Consciousness Academy running, where I offer my workshops and have many more ideas to keep developing people and raising humanity´s consciousness. This year I have also started my first Summit, the Global Consciousness Summit. I have developed myself as a business woman and have spoken at various events internationally, including London a few times and Hollywood, L.A. with the Phenomenal Global Woman project, where ten women decided to be the pioneers of the new paradigm change.

LOVE UNBOXED changed my life. I am empowered and free. My message for writing this chapter is to inspire women to be who they want to be. Nurture yourself so you don't need a relationship to make you feel complete. You want your new relationship to add something beautiful to an already fulfilled life, you don´t want your new partner to start telling you who to be or not to be.

WHAT NEXT: BELOVED CONSCIOUSNESS

I work to raise consciousness in the world and therefore, my own consciousness is the first one I work on. For relationship to raise consciousness it has to feel truly special, with someone who is on the same level of consciousness or even higher. Someone who will raise in love with me instead of falling in love with me. Someone with a strong spiritual connection. Someone who will love me and accept me as I am and who will bring out the best in me... the Beloved. We are talking about Beloved Consciousness.

Before I go into Beloved Consciousness, I will explain what I understand of Soul Mates and Twin Flames.

The Mind, which constantly seeks to name things, label every object, emotion and thought it encounters, needs to name those special relationships we regularly find with people who we feel that sort of wonderful connection with. We may feel we know the person from before, that we have known them all our lives, conversation is easy and if you are sensitive, you may even have visions of past lives with these people. There may be karma, positive or not, and the connection is strong. If the connection is intimate, the sexual attraction is very powerful.

This is what I understand of Soul Mates. People who come in and out of our lives with a distinctive affinity.

They don't stay forever. Once the karma is cleared and complete, they move on, always leaving a lesson and taking another. The Soul Mates are reflections of ourselves and after reflecting the good, they will reflect the not so good, bringing it up for healing.

The Twin Flame is the creation of the Mind for that special person that our Mind desires. The ideal partner who is our other half and completes us. The person who we will be sharing such magnificent love that will blind us.

These concepts are creations of the Mind and as such, bring us more despair and pain because of the great expectations we set up for this type of relationship.

The Beloved, though, is that person who has reached such a state of Consciousness that they see you as equal. Love is Pure and Unconditional. Physical presence is often always unnecessary.

My beautiful teacher Isis Livingstone taught us about Beloved Consciousness. She merged with her Beloved, a highly evolved spiritual being, and never met him in the flesh. She grew immensely and was happy with him. Her love story was lived by all who knew her. She received poems channelled from different sources and her Beloved was always there in spirit, by her side, supporting and loving her. The spiritual love is tangible yet not physical, it goes beyond body and mind and what the human can truly comprehend.

Once the Heart is opened and unburdened, once you live in JOY and emanate JOY from every ounce of your being, the Beloved can come near as it matches your frequency.

The Beloved is the One. The Beloved is the communion with the Divine. The Beloved is Merging with the Oneness of it all. We can merge with the Divine through another who is in the vibration of Pure Love. Although this is rare, it can happen.

The mystics of all times have reached blissful states of Consciousness by Devotion to the Beloved. The Communion with one's Soul, with the Unity of all that Is.

Living life in a Divine way, knowing oneself as God/Goddess while having a passionate and dedicated relationship with the Divine, in a Divine way. This leads to BLISS. Living for the Beloved transforms JOY into Divine BLISS. This is where we are heading toward in the new paradigm that we are bringing.

The Beloved brings Poetry, the yearning for the Infinite Union, the Understanding of Every-thing, the Un-Coding of the Unconscious, the Reprogramming of the Human Cells and the Reinvention of Love as we know it. This is Spiritual Technology. This is the point where Science meets Spirituality and becomes ONE.

Continuing my way towards self-realisation, this is what I am exploring now, the meeting and understanding of the Beloved in all levels of reality and all dimensions. But that is another story for another time in the New Paradigm... maybe for LOVE UNBOXED 3... where maybe, I will tell you about my Beloved.

CONCLUSION

My message is the same as in the first LOVE UNBOXED book, as it is so important, especially for us women: LOVE YOURSELF. It is through Love, through our open Heart that you can love another, only when you love yourself so fully that nothing matters but you. And you see yourself in every other Heart, in the Oneness of it all.

ABOUT THE AUTHOR

Born in Spain, Gema always felt a deep and inexplicable connection to the UK. When she turned 24 and she had gathered enough courage, she left everything behind and emigrated to England. She lived and worked in the UK for over 20 years. She made a career in IT Training and Change Management in the corporate world. At the same time, she studied spirituality and metaphysics, explored many healing techniques, attended workshops and lived with spiritual teachers who taught her about unconditional love, compassion and joy.

She now lives back in Spain and also in Glastonbury, UK.

She runs retreats and workshops to teach people about love and compassion, crucial qualities that everyone must incorporate into their skillset in order to thrive in the new world. She is passionate about Conscious Leadership and brings this new concept to countries and places where they are still operating in the old paradigm.

Gema dreams that everyone becomes a Conscious Leader during her time on Earth. From parents, to teachers, to students, to corporate leaders, to business owners, to world politicians and spiritual leaders... they all lead their lives and inspire other people one way or another. It is Gema´s dream that everyone awakens to the fact they are Creators of their own lives and Leaders of their destinies... when everyone becomes a Conscious Leader, with Conscious Awareness, LOVE and JOY find their way in... and they become FREE.

CONTACT

website: www.gemaramirez.com
www.globalconsciousnesssummit.com

LOVE UNBOXED: AN ANTHOLOGY BY WOMEN FOR WOMEN

PART TWO

SELF DISCOVERY, SELF LOVE AND HOPE

SLIMSPIRATION: LOSING DEADWEIGHT
Jenessa Qua: United Kingdom

"Whether you think you can or you can't, either way you are right."

~ Henry Ford 1863-1947

TIME TO LIVE

You cannot hear me
The silent scream inside
Can't know how it feels
To want to run and hide

From the pointing stares
And the shock in their eyes
The sniggering laughter
At my enormous size

Not about how much
Or how little I do eat
As deeper is my hunger
Wanting to feel complete

For it is just the symptom
Many years of the denial
I use as my protection
From more tears and trials

The constant contradiction
Forever fighting self
First loving then the loathing
My poor emotional health

Fresh new start is needed
Emerge from my cocoon
Like a beautiful butterfly
For me to truly bloom

A totally blank canvas
To rewrite and explore
Add awesome vibrant colours
To worship and adore

Time to take the challenge
Must be ready for the fight
Conquering my demons
To strive for better life

GROWING UP

'Ahow you look big so?!' In his laughing Jamaican voice, that was my Dad's greeting words when I got home from school. Used to his negative remarks, as usual I pretended not to hear. It was day 3 of not eating any food, (apart from an apple) in an attempt to reduce my large bust. So, on this occasion, his words stung. Life had always been difficult at home in my large family. My twin brother and I were the youngest born of 9 children, including two sets of twins.

Growing up in the 70's was a mixture of good, bad and traumatic times. I don't remember much about my childhood especially the younger years, as most of it I subconsciously blocked out. There were a couple of nice memories, but unfortunately the bad ones far outweigh the good. I was never sure of myself and felt confused and insecure, but mostly unlovable. It wasn't always easy to be heard amongst all my siblings. Although they'd say my brother and I were often treated like babies and spoiled. I learnt quickly how to get attention by being a good girl, then getting rewarded with extra food treats. I think that's when my distorted connection with food must have begun. When I did do something bad, it was frightening punishment with heavy licks from my strict Father's belt.

Even more painful to witness, was the terrifying beatings my poor Mother endured from a violent controlling husband. I would over eat to comfort myself, from living in the tense atmosphere of being on edge most of the time. Not knowing when or what the next explosive argument would lead to. I dreaded familiar sounds of tumbling, crashing, shouting and crying screams from my mother.

At school I was able to escape from all the madness at home. I loved singing and dancing, but felt awkward and different. Although I hated bringing attention to my large body, my school dance class gave me great joy of expression. At 12yrs old I had bigger breasts than all the girls in school, and hated wearing my awful 'Doreen' by Triumph, 34DD cup bra. Through my teens I continued to eat my way through depression. A few years later I discovered boys, or more accurately, they discovered me. I had my first boyfriend at age 15; he didn't seem to mind that I was fat. It was great at first but didn't last long as when my father found out, that was the end of that. He was actually brave enough to come to my house, to ask him if he could take me to a concert he'd bought tickets for. Of course, my father responded with a big fat 'NO!' I always thought I was undeserving and unworthy of love. So from then on, if I were ever lucky enough to have another boyfriend I'd do everything I could to please and keep him. The heartache of losing that first love hit hard and I began eating more to soothe the pain. Life was horrible. I couldn't wait to leave home, finally breaking out from the hell my father created aged 17.

ADULTHOOD

The following adult years was explored with naive eyes. I was inexperienced in the world and continued my comforting affair with food, to deal with responsibilities and stresses of daily solo life. For two years I studied dance at college and moved into a co-op community house for ten people. I never made it as a dancer. That world was far too body conscious for my size, where I stood out way too much. I then took various retail and office jobs, but the mundane reality of 9 to 5 couldn't stimulate my senses. Instead, it fuelled the empty loneliness I felt inside. By age 24 I had enough of my weight and foolishly tried slimming tablets. It took ten day's observation in hospital, after collapsing with erratic heart palpitations. The family were supportive, and my Mother was truly grateful I was alive, after previously losing one of my sisters from the result of a negligent hospital procedure. Having dropped so much weight in a matter of weeks, my never-ending abuse of food expanded my body further on return home.

I never had any male friends, always felt shy and awkward around them. We seldom mixed with boys in my small circle of girlfriends. When they approached me with complimenting advances, their interest melted my heart. My size never seemed to bother them, and the attention made me feel special. The next five years saw a few short-term boyfriends come and go. I was fat and unattractive, that's how I thought of myself. Very insecure and eager to please, so grateful to have someone I thought actually loved me. At age 29 after what I thought was a wonderful holiday romance, I returned home to find I was pregnant. He had no interest whatsoever in my predicament, and I never saw him again. I was stunned, disappointed and angry at myself. How could I let this happen? Just two days later, I had the shocking blow of my mother passing away, the only person that truly loved me. Life would never be the same again.

I couldn't tell you what it felt like to be pregnant as I was in total shock and denial the whole time. The devastation of losing Mum was overwhelming. Having an unplanned child by a guy I hardly knew, who didn't want anything to do with me, was mind boggling. I was in complete turmoil and didn't know what to do. My emotions were all over the place and the pressure of it all sent me spiralling out of control into a breakdown. I had a healthy baby boy and with the support of my family, I managed to get through the ups and downs of parenthood, to raise a wonderful son. I loved him dearly, but hated myself, how I looked and felt. I never did properly grieve for my mother, it now seemed like I had no one in the world; apart from my little boy who gave me unconditional love. I felt very alone, with food my only faithful companion. I had no time for anything as my child was now number 1 on the list. I neglected myself terribly and my health and wellbeing suffered. I ignored the signs for years, until my poor food choices, lack of exercise and heavy weight resulted in Type 2 Diabetes.

THE AWAKENING

After several previous attempts at losing weight, I vowed never again. I was afraid of yet another failure, but I so wanted to be slim and at last live a full healthy life. My son was now a teenager and would soon be going college. After all these years, I finally realised it was time to put ME first.

Sick and tired of fighting my bouts of depression, I wondered why my life was this way. Questions flooded my mind, but I had no answers and no one to turn to. It's hard to describe the wonderment of what happened to me next, but I can honestly say I felt my soul spirit energy reciting words to me, whispered from the Universe. I never was a good sleeper, but now my head was consumed with thousands of thoughts and feelings that seemed to overtake my mind, until I had to release them. I would jump out of bed as I thought my head would explode if I never recorded the transcript as given. I was used to writing songs, but this was something new, verses of words with no accompanying melody. Some so touchingly beautiful, that my heart wept with pure gratitude. It was January 2012 and I sensed a shift in the air. I felt lighter and happier at this new-found uplift. The only thing weighing me down was my heavy frame, now dress size 24 and 36L cup bra. I never weighed myself, but guessed I must've been around 16 stones. This was extreme and morbidly obese for my small height of 5'4".

I remember watching amazing weight loss transformation videos online for almost two years. Longing, I too would glowingly be happy, showing off my before and after photos. I liked the YouTube channel and joined their Facebook group. It was New Year's Eve 2011/12 when I received a surprise phone call. The male voice on the other end said, 'Let me help you change your life! His name was Laurence Brown, the consultancy he ran with his partner Sharon Myrie, was Dual Dynamics. They were the top of their field with the Cambridge Weight Plan. (CWP) Even after that first call, it still took me eight months to take the plunge and go for it 100%

I was nervous at meeting the legendary Laurence Brown at my first consultation. He was passionate about helping people and had a stern no nonsense approach. His excitable personality was infectious, and his partner Sharon was a beautiful dynamite Queen, who pulled no punches. They showed so much belief in me and knew I could do the program to great success. To me, they were like superheroes and soon became dear friends. The scales shouted an unforgiving 15st at me, and I was told my goal weight was 9st 7lbs.

I started on Step 1: Sole Source, which meant total meal replacement. I wanted to make a drastic change, and this certainly was that. The program entailed consuming high protein products, forcing your body to use its own fat for extra energy. This was scientifically known as setting your body into ketosis. My instructions were to; replace all three meals a day with these specially formulated packet foods and drink 3-4 litres of water. That was it, and then move up the steps. Slowly increasing calories and adding different food groups. Like a very long version of weaning a baby from liquids to solids. It made sense and was exactly what I needed, a complete rebirth.

From the very first meal, I couldn't believe how good all the products tasted. Days 1-3 were the hardest as my body adjusted to the minimal intake of calories and carbohydrates. I was determined to get through that first week, (as if I could manage that) I knew all I had to do was repeat the process. It was like a miracle, I found a totally focused mindset I never even knew was in me. On day 5, I was serving food for 120 people at my sister's surprise 50th Birthday party. Not once did I deviate from the plan. By day 7, I was euphoric at completing the first week and losing an astonishing 5lbs. That high remained throughout my whole journey. I started to believe I was worthy and deserved to live a happy healthy life. My perspective changed, and I gradually felt a new-found love and respect for myself. It may sound strange that changing your diet could do that, but it did.

The weeks went quickly, and the weight was melting off. By the second month people really noticed the difference. Surprisingly, some were not so happy with the new shrinking figure. There were only a handful of people fully behind me whilst dieting. It showed me how many flaky people and frenemies were in my life. I didn't care what anyone thought, I was on a mission. My solid as a rock consultants and new-found mindset was the biggest supporting factor towards my transforming body and life.

By month 4, I was over half way and could see the end in sight. I felt so proud and truly grateful to find patience and appreciation for every humble experience along the way. The little things like; thighs not chafing, a standard size bath towel wrapping around me, and for the first time actually seeing my crossed arms under my now smaller bust. Another amazing health benefit was my doctor reducing my tablets, until I was completely off all medication. My blood sugar levels were now in the normal range as a non-diabetic.

Whilst in my focused diet bubble, life still went on with all its wonderful highs and terribly devastating lows. November was the worse time for me. The walls in every room of my house were stripped to the brickwork, to repair gapping cracks from severe subsidence. Pure dust everywhere, it was like living on a building site, but I still managed my diet plan. Then my father was admitted to hospital because of complications with his failing kidneys. Within two weeks I watched him take his last breath.

They say that God never gives you more than you can cope with, and you never know how strong you are until you're faced with adversity. I was astonished at my resilience even when emotionally drained. My focus was stronger than ever, and I didn't eat one crumb throughout all my grieving. I know my dad would have been proud. He never liked a quitter and I was determined not to be one, in honour or his memory.

I continued to surpass my goal weight of 9st 7lbs, to become a size 8/10 at 9st 3lbs. I had photo shoots, a magazine article and best of all; my own

YouTube success story video. (https://youtu.be/vZor8erFGtA) It took seven months to lose 5st 10lbs. I loved my new slender petite frame and felt on top of the world. 6 months later, I was shortlisted for CWP Slimmer of the Year. I attended the Convention as a V.I.P guest. I never won, but in my mind, I was a successful winner from Day one.

CONCLUSION

When you really want something, and decide to love yourself enough to achieve it, you will always give your 100% best. I've learnt to love and believe in myself much more and that absolutely anything is possible, once you commit to your end goal. Just Believe!

ABOUT THE AUTHOR

In 2012, she had what she calls a Universal Upload, experiencing a compulsive urge to write. Creating four collections of poetry.

This led her to look at her unhappy life of childhood traumas, depression and obesity. To strive for positive change and discover a new joy of self-love

Her transformational journey opened her eyes and heart. Truly learning you can overcome and achieve anything you focus your mind to. She hopes her story will inspire others to do the same.

Jenessa is a single parent to one son. A performing artist who trained as a dancer, an Olivier Award winner and a first class vocalist. Working with top artists in the music industry, she regularly tours Europe with her own gigs and in theatrical productions.

CONTACT

Email: jenessaqua@gmail.com

TO FIND THE WAY HOME
Luna Miller: Sweden

Jump... And you will find out how to unfold your wings as you fall.

~ Ray Bradbury

Most people search for "the right place". Our mental, or maybe even more, emotional home. The place where we are totally appreciated and loved. Where there is always a kiss or a hug waiting for us. Where there is always a loving gaze meeting you wherever you turn your eyes. And for most of us women the searching is about finding a man. The man. The one and only.

I was looking for years and years. Finally, when I was in my late forties I found him. He loved, and still loves, every part of me. And I feel the same about him. We are totally different personalities. We have different needs. But together we make a balanced whole. Now. But it has not always been like that. For many years parts of me were still unhappy and insufficient.

THE FOG

When we first met he lived in another city than me. It took about three hours by train or car. So, we met during weekends. In one way, it was a nice time. I love adventures. And to travel by train, up north, was an adventure for me. At that time, I also really needed the peace and quiet of the countryside. For the first time, since my childhood, I had access to a house with a big garden and a lovely little greenhouse that I called "The conservatory". It became the heart of that place for me. My space. Where I could just sit and let the thoughts drift. Inviting my man for a glass of champagne on Friday afternoons. But mostly being there by myself. Taking care of the flowers. Or just be.

At the same time, this period was hard on me. Travelling back and forth demanded a lot of energy and money. It was also heart-breaking to be with my new love for intense weekends and then apart during the week. My love was not much about talking on the phone so for me, who loves to talk a lot, that was a bit hard to get used to as well.

When we, after two years, got married we finally moved in together. I was so happy. Convinced that everything would be perfectly fine now. The "happy ever after"-thing. And yes, love has been good. We have had each other. But happy? No. We have both been struggling with demons and both became lost on different paths in the darkest of worlds.

My husband has no problems finding jobs. But he has had difficulty enjoying them, which results in him changing jobs often. At the time, when we moved together, head hunters used to call him. I was really envious about this, because I felt stuck in my job. I had been at the same place for years and was longing for something else. I did apply for other jobs, but there were not that many that were suited to me. And I did not get the few that there were.

For many years I had worked with people that were close friends as well. But suddenly they were all gone. Moved to new jobs and I was stuck. Feeling unsuccessful. At that time, there were conflicts going on at work. Conflicts I could not do anything about except let it eat me. It was a pain to go to work. It seemed like everyone was angry or unhappy. I wanted nothing else but to leave. At the same time knowing that wanting to leave is not the best route to a new job.

The best way is to know where you want to go. But I had no idea where I wanted to go, except for getting away from the current painful situation. And it was not only about the job. Looking back at that time is sad. It was like I was stuck in thinking of all the bad things and focusing on what I did not have: a lot of money; time to write; a fit body; a job that did not take all my energy and so on.

I made a big effort to try and concentrate on myself. Doing things, I love. Like writing. I have wanted to be an author for the whole of my life. I had the time and space, but it was like I did not let myself. I was stuck in my own drama always finding other things that were more important to do first, such as cooking and cleaning and sacrificing myself to the work by working late hours. Over and over again.

And then my husband got cancer.

LOST

I fell and fell and fell into the darkness. And still I had to stand straight. Be strong, be comforting, be the one that understood and remembered doctor´s instructions. Be the one that sat beside and helplessly watched when the Cytotoxin affected the loved one. Be the one that took care of the household. Be the one to sits beside them, day after day, hoping for the loved one to get better. At the same time, be the one that knew that it would take time. Not being able to help or provide relief.

I made an agreement with my job to only work four days a week so that I could spend the weekend and one weekday with my husband. Be there for him. Except for the days of treatment at the hospital, he spent most time in bed alone. My emotional tentacles grew long. I could feel every mood shift of his. When he had a good day, I was happy hoping for the best. But for a long time, the good days was the easiest to count. And suddenly I knew more about his emotions than of my own. I lost myself.

It was a hot summer when he got ill. We had been only a few days on holiday when the scary message arrived, and we had to head back home for his treatment. We were stuck in the apartment because we were both to full of fear and anxiety to be around other people. So, I spent most of that summer in the shade at the balcony with my feet in a bucket filled with cold water.

This is when I finally gave myself time to write. For all my life, I have had this picture of me as a writer.

And yes, I have been writing from time to time. But I never had the patience nor the energy to complete a story. I had never given myself the space to really work through my book projects. But now I had the time and the big need to find myself an oasis. With feet in the bucket and the laptop on the balcony table in front of me, I started my own journey.

I did not write about myself. I wrote about fictional women and the need to make good choices in life. The need of putting oneself first, to be able to love and respect others. That your dreams are important whatever they are. I wrote about the disasters that can look you up if you let them, if you don´t watch your own back. The love between people is fantastic but hard to fully enjoy if you don´t love yourself.

During this hot summer and the autumn that followed I wrote two books. And I published them myself. The writing became my safe and happy space. And secret. It took a long time before I told anyone except my closest. The feeling was that I really wasn´t allowed. I was scared that people would read and hate the books. I felt so fragile that I feared any kind of criticism.

It was clear that I was not well at all. When I finally contacted the health care centre the doctor diagnosed me as depressed. In a way, I was relieved to understand that there was a name for the state I was in. That it was a state that could change. But then the doctor told me to get hold of myself. That nobody wants a depressed mother or wife. That I should buy myself some flowers and some clothes with colours and just snap out of it.

This was a total shock for me. And degrading. But the worst thing was that I believed her. So, I did not tell anyone about this for a long time. I was too ashamed. I carried it in my heart, feeling that I was not worthy of love when I was depressed. That I had to be happy, being the one to take care of everything with a smile and not demanding anything for myself.

When I finally shared the story with others of my catastrophic meeting with the doctor I realized, by their reactions, that I had been offended in a way that was not okay. That made me realize that I had to learn to stand up for myself. One way of doing this was to tell friends that I was an author. And when I finally started to tell people about my writing it was well received. Not only that, I realized that when you tell people about your passion and dreams you open a special door inside even for them.

So, the writing finally got me on a good track. When I created that space I started a new phase in my life. A phase full of love and adventure. And with me feeling good about myself I started to appreciate my work and my colleagues in a way I had not done for a long time. I found joy in being at work, doing the best I could, realizing that I could manage to do my duties without sacrificing my leisure or getting into conflicts. And when I no longer felt this intense longing to be away from that job, I was offered an even better job. I chose the new job after a lot of thinking, because it would give me more time to be an author. More time to follow my dream.

WHEN CLOUDS LIGHTEN

I do not claim that becoming a writer is the solution for everybody. But it sure was for me. It was my way of teaching myself to know. For real. It was my way of finding a safe platform, my oasis, where I could feel safe enough to have a closer look at myself. And most of all – loving myself. Accepting my lesser impressive sides. Being able to smile at myself, thinking that it is ok if I am too fat, if I sometimes talk too much or say the wrong things. I am still an adorable woman who is mostly made of love. The other parts, I think, will be healed by having access to all that love, now, when I don´t feel ashamed about them.

I have learned so much from the characters I write about. Learned so much about myself and my way of thinking and feeling. Their destinies are results of my inner wisdom. It is my gift to the world. And my gift to myself.

It is hard to be a human. And it is hard to be a woman. But it is also totally wonderful from time to time. And it is so much easier if you love and appreciate yourself. And the best way to do that is to let yourself spend time alone doing what you are passionate about. During many years I had all the focus on other people, forgetting about myself. The biggest problem with that kind of typical female behaviour is that you create negative needs. A need to get something more than just love back from the persons you focus on. There is a big risk of becoming a drama queen. Because giving "everything" to another person is not good for any of you if that means that you will give up on yourself. I know that my husband neither has asked me, nor wanted me to give up my dreams for him. Quite the opposite.

AND LIFE GOES ON

Love is a fantastic healing power and a great adventure that I wish for all people to experience. But I think it is important for all women out there to remember that no man can totally replace the dreams of your own. But he can be a fantastic travel companion on the journey against them.

To wrap up my story – my husband is well again, and he is by my side. I have some dreams that are only mine and I am working to fulfil them. But we also have dreams together. So, side by side we are slowly finding our way home.

ABOUT THE AUTHOR

I have always known that my ambition in life was to be a writer, and still it took so long before I gave it a fair chance. I did do some writing during those years but did not give it enough time or care.

When I published my first book two years ago I was terrified, scared of what other people would think, that they would not like it. But as time passed the passion and joy of writing healed me.

It became my sunny island in the eye of the storm. My writing took me on voyages to other worlds, to places where my characters could live, love, fight and screw up.

The loved and the infuriating, the nice and the mean. The ones that know their way and the ones that get lost. Characters that go their own way but allow me to follow their adventures. The fate and stories of people who struggle to get it right, as we all do.

I am no longer afraid of what people think of my books. But of course, it warmed my heart when I got some fantastic reviews this summer and made it to the bestseller list. But the best thing is all the stories still left inside of me, eager to come to life.

CONTACT

Website: www.Lunamiller.com
Email: Lunamiller.writer@yahoo.com

FOODIE IN THE MAKING
Christine Smith: Australia

William Shakespeare said, "the meaning of life is to find your gift – the purpose of life is to give it away"

UNDER THE INFLUENCE

When I look back over my life I can see that my gift is the ability to share my passions of food and the development of people achieving what is important to them. From the age of fifteen whilst attending high school in Singapore I volunteered on Saturdays at a local primary school teaching English, to working with the long term unemployed whilst working in employment services and now in my NFP community kitchen, Recipe4Change, based in Melbourne, Australia, sharing is always at the forefront.

So where did my sense of social justice come from?

Probably my father, a career Royal Marine. I grew up in England and Singapore & believed I had a normal childhood. Well it was normal to me; stable home, loving parents, food on the table, decent clothes and footwear though there was not an excess of spare money. My Mum was a good budgeter.

I didn't experience domestic violence or drunkenness.

Then, two years ago I met Susan, she said I had a privileged upbringing. Susan had family, but experienced on many occasions, hunger, loneliness and isolation.

Perception is everything isn't it?

LOVE UNBOXED

What we are really talking about here is the hunger to belong, be loved and encouraged, not just food.

When I analysed what my father fostered in me, it was a sense of self-worth with unwavering self-belief by letting me learn life's lessons in a safe and nurturing environment.

So why is my life so full of food today? For me food evokes so many wonderful memories and looking back, my life adventures have been built around food or what happened in the kitchen. Some of my happiest memories involve food. No wonder my life centres round food - I am now known as the Food Warrior.

Just this week someone asked what was my first memory of food?

I remember a warm sunny day in the summer of 1960, sitting on a blanket in the garden with my brothers, having a picnic tea. We ate cold meat, boiled eggs and salad & bread spread with real butter followed by tinned fruit. If you grew up in the UK in the 50's & 60's then you would remember the Mr Wippy soft serve ice cream van. Every day he came around and if it was tea time we went and got a bowl of ice cream to have with tinned fruit. One shilling fed the whole family.

I was 9yrs old when we bought our first fridge. Houses we lived in had dark cold larders and you ate fresh food. What wasn't fresh came in a can like Spam or ham and fruit. Nothing was wasted, leftovers became the base of next day's dinner.

We always ate as a family at the table. At a dinner table, many of life's lessons are learned. It's where we learned - manners. We learnt to share, to listen and the art of conversation. "The family meal is the nursery of democracy" as the saying goes.

Even in play food featured. I was either scrumping apples, picking blackberries along a country lane or sharing afternoon tea with friends. One of those friends, Alyson is my longest friend, of 54 years and she lives in a house that was on my paper round as a 14 yrs. old.

Whilst I learnt to cook, sew and knit from my Mum, family will tell you I am "My father's daughter". We shared a passion for good food, jigsaw puzzles, reading and practical skills like woodwork and decorating.

Growing up in the era after the war, ration books still existed as food was not plentiful unless you grew it yourself. There were not the proliferation of supermarkets, takeaway shops and cafes like today. My parents and maternal grandparents all grew veggies and fruit. My favourite aunt and uncle, Rod and Gill still maintain a very productive vegetable patch after giving up their allotment.

Mum's parents lived in Plymouth where she met Dad. Another thing that we share is finding a way to make things happen. He forged his mum's signature, so he could sign up under age. I loathe institutional thinking, for me rules are guidelines only.

Gran Lee's dining room table was always covered with a fresh table cloth, with a board of an uncut loaf of bread, jam made from her own garden offerings and a tin of Devon clotted cream. Her pasties were legendary, boats to be devoured with brown sauce. I use my gran's plate, fork & knife to make my own. Supper times at the end of a day's play were a treat, with 6 pence we bought a bag of hot chips-something we never had at home – takeaway food.

My Dad's family lived where I was born in Doncaster, Yorkshire. My Gran lived across the road from the railway sidings where my Uncle Jimmy had an allotment. To this day when I pick a homegrown tomato I am transported back to the day he took me to the allotment.

Has a similar experience happened to you? How did you feel?

Breakfasts were fried egg, bacon and fried bread cooked in an inch of dripping. Some days I still yearn for fried bread.

In 1967 we moved to Singapore which opened up a whole new world of food. Nasi Goreng or hot chips at school for lunch washed down with a frozen bottle of coke. Dating Pete a Royal Marine, gave me entre to the night life including Bogey Street with amazing food and sneaky alcoholic drinks. I learned to bargain fairly and be respectful of the many different cultures. Coming from a white England the move was a cultural shock, but one soon replaced with wonder and respect.

School boyfriends were special and today I am still in contact with many friends of that extra special time in my life. We are known as Brit Brats and as a military child we have our own poem which will give you an insight into why my life has unfolded as it has:

"As a Military Child the Dandelion is our official flower, as it puts down roots almost anywhere and is almost impossible to destroy. It's an unpretentious plant, yet beautiful and strong.

It's a survivor in a broad range of climates.

Military children bloom everywhere as the wind carries the family.

They are hardy and upright.

Their roots are strong, cultivated deeply in the culture of the military.

They are ready to fly in the breezes that take them to new adventures, new lands, and new friendships.

Experts say that military children are well-rounded, culturally aware, tolerant, and extremely resilient.

Military children have learned from an early age that home is where the heart is, that a good friend can be found in every corner and culture of the world, and that education doesn't only come from school.

They ideally live history!

They learn that to survive means to adapt, that the door closes with one chapter of their lives and opens up to a new and exciting adventure full of new experiences."

Rhonda who lived across the road in Singapore reminded me just this week of bottles of coke with aspirins in at the dockyard dances. My second lifelong friend is Jane who I met the first school day at St John's. We meet up around the world as we have travelled and settled.

Back in the UK for a short time before moving to Australia I met my future husband Trevor who introduced me to the life in London, heady days where you would pass Marianne Faithful and Mick Jaggar and think nothing of it. In March 1971 we moved to Adelaide. We had come from a life in Singapore of open doors and windows to locked front doors and closed windows with neighbours who initially wouldn't speak to us because they thought we were Spanish gypsies. We felt trapped.

Trevor was my chief taste tester and endured many cooking experiments. I remember the first time Mum & Dad came to lunch. I cooked a roast successfully and my prized apple pie had inch thick pastry – top, bottom and sides. Trevor today cooks a mean chilli con carne & is the best oven cleaner I know.

We have two wonderful kids Kirsty and Kristian who have forged their own lives in which food also figures. Kirsty works in hospitality and though prefers not to cook, produces a mean apricot chicken. Her daughter loves to bake. Kristian cooked his first meal when he was 4 and went on to be a chef. Both of his children love to spend time in the kitchen with him. Mum at 85 stills cooks her meals.

AUSSIE ENTREPRENEUR

In 1997 I upped sticks and moved to Melbourne beginning a journey that led me to what I do today. In my opinion Melbourne is the centre of Australia's food scene. They say there are enough eating houses, so every person can eat out at the same time. A new friend labelled me a trencher man, he was in awe of the amount of food I could eat. We won't mention my love of good wines.

I worked in job services and again that "rules are only guidelines" popped up and I started a breakfast program for single socially isolated men who then learnt to cook and become independent.

In 2000 I travelled to Italy for a month of food and wine and discovered Limoncello, now my secret ingredient in my cheesecakes. Shhhh don't let the secret out.

2001 was a gut-wrenching year with my first grandson diagnosed with Leukemia in the March, losing my corporate job and then my Dad died on 1ST September, the day before Father's Day. I felt like I had lost my rudder. My Dad wasn't perfect, but he was a strong influence in my life even after being diagnosed with Parkinsons around the time he retired. I retreated from a working life unable to deal with people including my own family. Daniel survived and has grown into a lean considerate young man living life to the fullest.

After taking my doctor's advice, I sought counselling which helped me move through my grief. I bought a van, became a courier and slowly worked my way back into corporate life. I recognised I was a different person and again the lessons my father taught me came to the fore and I recommenced working with job seekers, which also helped me mend and back into self-employment.

In 2011 I started Rowville Community Kitchen as a social enterprise & in 2014 registered as a NFP starting a work experience program based around simple wholesome cooking, showing job seekers how to save money by planning and cooking easy meals. And sharing all the life lessons I unknowingly learnt along the road called life including lessons learnt from my father: Set boundaries, do not judge, give everyone a fair go, be true to your values and be congruent.

While focussing on the United Nations Sustainability Development Goals:

No poverty 2. Zero hunger 3. Good health and wellbeing 5. Gender equality 10. Reduce inequalities & 12. Responsible consumption and production, we exist solely to serve and connect our local community in Knox.

How? We make meals that matter.

We share our extensive skills and excess surplus produce from local suppliers to provide knowledge, cooking skills and wholesome meals cooked from scratch. We engage our local Knox community through Work for the Dole programs, cooking classes in primary schools, Thursday's restaurant quality community lunches for our most vulnerable seniors & a marketplace fresh produce table stocked with surplus produce from local suppliers that support families experiencing tough times.

Food and cooking breaks down barriers and brings fun into people's lives. We make meals that matter – we bring together different parts of our local community to address the critical issue of food insecurity where people don't have access to nutritional food for an active healthy life, especially primary school students, so they can learn, grow and participate fully in school

With 64% of primary school students attending with empty stomachs our number one aim is to eradicate food poverty in our local primary schools so we partner with seven primary schools, providing sandwiches, fresh fruit and veg to share and meals for the families of students experiencing domestic violence, poor mental health and under employment.

Kitchen scraps feed chooks, the worm farm at the men's shed or go to compost.

I especially love desserts, experimental cooking & entertaining friends. Who needs an excuse to celebrate good food and great company?

Solo travel is another passion, mostly staying in apartments so I can immerse myself with the locals. There is nothing better than the local cafe putting your choice coffee on the counter as you walk in the door ……oh to be back in Paris. Or to share a glass of wine with the local store owner in country Italy at the end of the day: homemade of course.

Life in the kitchen is busy everyday so I always have a jigsaw puzzle on the table at home, unfortunately I become so engrossed I forget the time and to eat.

In warmer months there is nothing so relaxing at the end of the day sitting on my back decking with a cuppa, talking to a couple of cockatoo who frequent my backyard to discuss our day or hang over the back fence with June and a glass of red.

As CEO the buck stops with me for budgeting, negotiations, meeting deadlines and delivering information to our stakeholders. My role as mentor to job seekers is to influence & assist them transition out ready for work so they can make informed decisions and find their own pathway to success.

As leader of my team of two, I encourage questions and creative solutions to our daily challenges. Whilst chef is an awesome culinary manager he readily admits he can't work spreadsheets and dislikes talking to people.

Joanne, my admin assistant, a single Mum who after five years, has just moved on to other challenges. We joke that I taught her all I know, and she has perfected my bad habits. Not only did she learn to cook from scratch during her employment, her son is also cooking,

My greatest strength is in networking and building strategic alliances. One business owner said "you know how to push the right buttons to get a solution". I agree. I know how to deliver the same information to different stakeholders to gain the best outcomes for Recipe4Change.

ABOUT THE AUTHOR

Christine is known as a food warrior and advocate for social justice. Whilst the focus of her business is providing a "hand up" there is still much concern about the level of handouts provided without consideration to empowering families to break the cycle of food poverty and have choices in the food they eat. Christine would argue she is not political, cooking it seems is a political act.

Michael Pollan said "Cooking is what happens between farming and eating. It's a political act, he suggests, because by cooking we can improve our health, break our dependence on conglomerates, and build community". Christine's goal for the next year is to hold workshops and retreats so other women can learn to dig deep, find their true reason for being in this life and live their passion every day.

CONTACT

Website: www.christinepsmith.com.au
Email: christine@christinepsmith.com.au

WHAT SIZE?
Dr Arinola Araba: United Kingdom

"A life lived on purpose is the most fulfilling and potentially impacting to the world around me"

~ Arinola Araba

SHOE SIZE MATTERS!

"I want to be a boy," I repeatedly told my mum. And her usual reply was, "go on, be a boy!" As I grew up, so did my feet and chest size making me a misfit for the usual shoe and dress shops for my age then.

There was a common belief amongst gynaecologists that women with large feet possessed a bigger pelvis, wide enough to make the passage of a baby during delivery easier. The bigger feet did not really work in my favour when I went looking for shoes, larger than size 8 in English standards.

I always struggled to find good bras too, since my chest was quite voluminous. Welcome to my world of trying to and yet not really fitting in to the world around me.

Did I really have to stand out?

With the sound of laughter, I still find a way to see the humour in the most challenging of situations and I still look for opportunities to fit my 10 toes and body into!

BEFORE MY BEGINNING

Born as first child into an exciting family in the famous African town called Lagos in West Africa, I came into the world with surprises.

My mum says I refused to come out on my expected delivery date, arriving when I was overdue, thereby making my delivery a little more troublesome for mum.

She recounts that she had to shout along with the womb contractions, so the midwives knew exactly when she was getting those pain waves so from their offices, the sound from mum made it easier for them to record the progress of labour without visiting her bed side.

By the time I was ready to be born, mum was exhausted from all the vocal and bodily responses she had made during the preparation of the womb for my delivery!

You will appreciate that so much happened after, much of which I am not aware of - obviously, as I'm only recounting what mum has told me.

LAUGHTER, SO NECESSARY

Apparently, I was a happy baby who loved dancing! Mum says that whenever she was feeding me in the baby chair I would stop taking the spoon of food unless she sang me a song.

So, the song in Yoruba (Nigerian):

Arinola Ori se se, ijo lo fe ma jo, bata lo fe ma wo, owe lo fe ma ka...

In my Anglicised translation, it means, All Arinola wants to do is dance, play and read books!

BE MINDFUL OF WHAT YOU SAY!

The power of those words has underpinned my life's journey. I am so playful you would not believe I was working if you came to my office base. You would think my life and work was one big comedy.

Well! It has come with many benefits and has probably resulted in some doors being shut in my face. So much for my so happy-go-fun way of doing things, but it allows me to make friends easily just as much.

Another incident in my childhood springs to mind. Mum would sit at one end of the dining table and ask me time and time again why I stared at her. Why? I wanted a reaction. Countless times, I would stop eating to look at mum with a quizzical glare. She told me later, she always wondered what I was thinking and why I constantly stared at my fingers.

MATHS FINGERS

It seemed as if I had a 'bad' habit if doing maths every time someone around me spoke. I was so fascinated by words and the numbers of letters that they were made of. I had a habit of comparing the number in letters for different sentences and phrases.

So, I learned to do maths from an early age. I enjoyed reading and writing too. To lay the foundation for the path I have taken in life, there are still a couple of stories to relate to you.

There was a plant on the coffee table in the sitting room that always grabbed my attention and finger's grip too. I would play with the green leaves and on occasion snap them, much to mum's annoyance. She would tell me off for playing with the plant telling me to leave it alone, but that only served to encourage me to play more.

On one occasion, she had tapped me lightly on the hand as a warning to stop this ′plant habit′. In return I had taken mum's hand, touched the plant with it, then tapped her hand in the same manner I think she had mine. I suppose this was one of many sample lessons in assertion, reasoning and acting out my many thoughts.

When people say, "may your road be rough" I sometimes wonder if it's wrong. Because if my life is anything to go by, I do not think good times ever lasted for long enough for me to hold onto! As if anyone could?

I remember a conversation with my mum just after I turned 21, as a medical doctor. She lamented the fact that things always seemed to go so hard for me in life and she could never understand it.

LOSS OF CONTROL

I grew up in what was then known as a broken home and lived with my dad. It was so tough growing into my teen years without a loving mum to show me what a lady looked, acted and dressed like. So, I think a lot of what I learned came from outside the family - media, friends and other relatives.

The pain of mum and dad's reaction to the separation took its toll on us four kids. There were times when all we would do was watch TV, bake, cook and eat, so I kept getting fat to my dad's annoyance. I was sporting a dress size 12/14 around the time I was 14 years old. I even thought that dress sizes were equal to age at time.

My dad's angry comment about my size (weight) and being out of control when he bought me a stretchy dress and threw it at me, broke the eating spell. I suddenly became aware of how big I was getting. I think food was filling a void created by the pain and loneliness of not having a resident parent to confide in.

Life was very far from easy in our household and burying myself in school work, assignments, reading and more work filled the void for a while, until I was introduced to an invisible friend - God.

In a casual conversation with a friend at a boarding school, I gave my life over to God and He became my best friend. Like someone who was in love and loved, I would sing all the time and I think that must have earned me a place in the school choral group too.

BOY, DID I GROW UP?

Boarding school was over 600km from our Lagos home and not a ready or popular choice for my parents as 'they' spoke a different Nigerian language to the Yoruba I was more conversant with. The decision to allow me to wander to uncharted territory was a tough one and my mum, I think agonised at that time over how she could trust me to look after myself at the age of 10. I still recall her comments then about how difficult I would find it to take care of my clothes, brush my teeth and keep my hair in tidy shape. It was settled I had to cut my hair - short. It's funny that at 50, I now wear my hair short.

Anyway, it was finally agreed that I would go to school far away, meaning that I would get some sort of 'freedom' to be me. What did that even mean?

In my head at the time, I thought the rules that governed our home were too tough, so I expected that I was going to a place where it would be easier.

You can imagine my shock when I discovered there were rules to be obeyed and punitive measures for straying out of line - oh dear.

I was called the girl in green, because I regularly wore one of the three dresses allowed in school on most weekends, before we were issued school dresses. By the time the latter happened, the 'girl in green' title had time to stick.

It was after my departure to boarding school that things came to a head at home. I had not realised how bad the situation was until a letter arrived and in very graphic detail, described to me how my mum had been beaten to stupor.

She was later admitted to hospital as an emergency because she was being kicked, and lay on the floor in blood at the mercy of her abuser. It was a neighbour who organised her treatment.

I could have lost my mum!

She came through that ordeal and became a pivotal support to me much later in life when I was faced with a similar situation in my marital home, 20 years later.

GROW UP GIRL

History repeats!

I completed boarding school in lower secondary school, then started A levels. Then, there were opportunities to apply to university at the GCSE level, so I took advantage of this and received admission to study a biological science. That was not exactly what I was aiming for, but I was happy to go to university rather than stay for two years of A' levels.

I fast tracked into higher education, switched courses to study Medicine and Surgery and was well on my way to success in life, until...

AFTER MED SCHOOL

Somehow it did not feel like I was sitting on top of the world after completing medical school. I still felt something was missing.

In my quest to find answers, I decided it was time to travel abroad for a holiday. Little did I know how long that journey would take.

It would lead me to a marriage, parenthood, further study, separation, divorce, debt, unemployment, hardship, enterprise and innovation; but not necessarily in that order.

THE WESTERN CALL

I arrived in the UK hyper excited for a change in my world. It was very difficult to understand the thinking of another culture and to get around the meaning of words that I had previous been used to using in conversation.

The words 'help me' was an admission that I needed support and assumed the recipient would instinctively understand what type of help I was requesting, except in the UK. And what about people saying to you, 'say again' because they wanted you to repeat what you were saying because they could not understand your accent!

Then there was a more cruel comment when people say, "you are mumbling," "you need to speak up!"

Extraordinarily I met someone who said, very deliberately, "I need to meet with you face to face because I do not understand your accent when you are on the phone!"

A DIFFERENT KETTLE OF FISH

Work is essential

There were other experiences where I would apply for a job, get it, then endure the farce of having to train a new employee who would then take my job.

The world of jobs ended when I decided to take a jump from the security of a permanent contract to a temporary one. It started with a maternity cover for a year and turned into me signing up as a consultant to the health service. I had the most exciting opportunity to move from one health trust to another, helping with staff training, monitoring and quality assurance.

By this time, I had achieved a first-class degree, other IT and management courses and a Masters in

Health Informatics. The latter became handy when I was problem solving and analysing trends for incidents and risk management strategies (health speak, sorry)!

Strangely enough, some of these short-term contracts ended in March. And I was beginning to get restless after about four years of consulting.

The ending of the last contract was quickly followed by a worrying spell of very little income driving me to yet another period of anxiety. I began to feel a pull towards volunteering as this appealed to me at a time when I needed a reason to get out of the house.

A BUSINESS IS BORN

An application to a community facility hub offering opportunities to people wanting to create solutions to social problems was more than just appealing- it was an outlet for my frustrating lack of activity and being needed.

bMoney Wize Ltd became the result of a search to solve real life problems that affect us all - managing finances.

By this time, I had become a casualty of that not much-talked-about problem - debt. It served as a propeller for the next exciting phase of my life.

Money was in short supply and my very generous daughter would bring her friend's home for an after school cook up as she was learning those essential skills - preparing meals.

Well, when it dawned on me that it was my place to teach my daughter financial skills, I suddenly developed a new energy. The type that keeps you awake with ideas and possibilities of what could be done. We rounded up 22 teenagers, ranging in age from 12 to 19 and asked them a question:

How can we make teaching money, fun and engaging for kids?

We got more than what we asked for because the outcome of that question resulted in the creation of a globally recognised maths skills board game - bmoneywize.

Uniquely bmoneywize www.bmoneywize.co.uk

Some parents have described it as: http://www.goodtoknow.co.uk/family/547717/bmoneywise-game-aims-to-boost-kids-financial-awareness.

We got to the global awards for innovative higher education pedagogies enhancing learning and employability http://bit.ly/2qCRUzK

We think it's a refreshing new approach to helping kids with their financial literacy and numeracy skills.

Bmoneywize is a fun and engaging game that is also educational. It introduces the complex concepts of financial literacy to kids in a way that is simple and opens up a dialogue between them and their parents about money.

The game breaks down the consequences of the decisions to spend frivolously in a way that is easy to understand and how this can be prevented. The scenarios that are explained are every-day and mostly commonplace. They were carefully picked to depict the lifestyle of the average person, and while humourous are also very relatable.

Awards / Nomination for board game

- Best new product - Corporate Entrepreneur Awards 2015

- Barking & Dagenham Business Innovation 2013 & 2016

- arc Start Up Competition Winner – Business in the Community, 2013

- Shortlisted for Reimagine Education Awards, USA, Dec 2016

The maths game received daily press reviews in the Daily Mail? http://dailym.ai/2eMD6xB and the Sunday Times http://bit.ly/2fdlxqL. A game class looks like this: http://bit.ly/2w9fVo6

CONCLUSION

Troubles in life come to disguise many opportunities uniquely suited to you!

All troubles do come to pass...eventually. We either get used to them, find a solution for them or they get resolved. Like me, you may cry a little...

So, take heart, dear one, dear reader, your future is ahead of you and it's looking brighter.

ABOUT THE AUTHOR

You cannot forget an encounter with that 50 year-old-turning 35, boisterous mum to 3 young adults, 18, 20 and 21 who bounces as she walks.

She sings and dances on the side streets and public transport; a fun, lively and engaging character with a smile. She always has a kind word to say, that is Arinola, coach, blogger, inventor of an educational board game and multi award nominee, socio-entrepreneur.

And she has bigger than usual feet!

CONTACT

Website: www.arinola.co.uk
Email: arinola@bmoneywize.co.uk

RAINBOW BEHIND THE CLOUDS
Kimberley Armstrong: United States

"I truly believe that everything we do and everyone that we meet is put in our path for purpose"

~ Marla Gibbs

THIS IS WHERE IT ALL BEGAN

Throughout my lifetime, I have been involved in numerous love stories. Unfortunately, too many were filled with heartbreak, and coupled with one rejection after another. The reasons for my repeated rejection came in many forms. Either, I was not pretty or glammed up enough, or too statuesque, opinionated, passionate, independent, or too nurturing. Although heartache was prevalent in my life, there is one story which counters and overshadows the pain that rejection brings. That love came in the unexpected and unconditional love of my Aunt Aretha.

Standing at a mere five feet tall, her petite stature belied her grand presence. The woman that I affectionately refer to as Momtee has aged quite gracefully for her ninety-two years of age and experience. I created her name, Momtee because it was a combination of Mom and Auntie. By blood, she is my great-aunt. However, in my eyes she is my Mother. And if anyone were to ask her, she would readily declare that I am her daughter. Although she didn't carry me in her womb, endure pregnancy with its myriad of inconveniences such as morning sickness and labor pains, she has since carried me in her heart for over three decades.

One summer when I was a child, my Mom began helping my great aunt take care of my uncle Mac because he was dying from cancer. In the evenings, Mom worked at a nearby hospital caring for patients. It was a passion she meticulously took pleasure in and everyone knew she put a great deal of heart with it. Because she had a great relationship with my aunt and uncle, they felt content having someone they could trust who was also family providing his nursing care needs. My siblings and I went with my Mom every day when she took care of him. As she busily worked on him, Uncle Mac would repeatedly and quizzically tell my mother that he saw something different in me.

He said it looked as if I had a lot of stuff on my mind for one so young. Then he would follow up with saying that I was smart as a whip and sharp as a tack. Uncle Mac would routinely inquire out loud, "I really see something in Kim, she is hiding all this good stuff inside of her and holding on to it. When she does decide to let it go she will be a talker for sure. I tell you she has a plenty to say." To this day, I wonder how he saw me, really saw me because I was an incredibly shy, bashful and withdrawn seven-year-old little girl hiding behind a wall of shame. I felt trapped on the inside and was screaming for help, but was unaware of how to get it.

My being headstrong was frequently mistaken for rebellion. As the years went by, I learned to be tight-lipped about everything because when I did share my truths, there was always the consequences of chastising adults declaring that I was "too grown" for my age. To the contrary, Uncle Mac always praised me and everything he said to me was positive. He would continually make pronouncements over my future about how I was going to make a huge impact one day on people who were rejected and walked over. I can still hear his gentle voice telling me how beautiful and smart I was. And because I could not see those positive attributes about myself, his words left me feeling awkward because I thought he pitied me.

Over the years, I could not help but wonder if Uncle Mac knew the painful secret I was carrying. To this day, I never got the answer to that question. One of the most amazing things about Uncle Mac was that he was everyone's caring uncle in both our community and church. He always carried jars filled with candy for the kids, and made a point to encourage them all to be the best at everything regardless of their circumstance. He would go out of his way to make people laugh, and if he knew one of the community kids had something going on at school he and my aunt made a point to personally attend ball games, plays, speeches, or any extracurricular activity especially if the children's parents could not attend, to make everyone feel special.

As we watched him go through the five stages of dying, Uncle Mac thanked my Mom over and over for her selfless sacrifice on his behalf. As the days of his life narrowed to a close, he asked my Mom to grant him a dying wish that she would allow me to stay with his wife, my Aunt Aretha after he passed away. He wanted me to be her companion because they never had children of their own, although they nurtured and guided a village of children over the years supporting both their educational needs and personal well-being.

Dear Uncle Mac took exquisite care of my Aunt Aretha. He took care of all the bills and anything pertaining to the house while she maintained the domestic needs inside the home. Even as he prepared to depart this earthly realm, he tirelessly prepared by leaving my aunt detailed instructions in a notebook of when the bills were due, how to pay them and who to call when she needed repairs. The notebook carried crucial dates for when the insurance, light, gas, and water bills were due. Inside of this little notebook of love and care contained all the information to the plumber, electrician, yard person, and any other thing you could of thought might go wrong and need fixing. I remember my aunt refer to that manual of love frequently after Uncle Mac passed.

Before his passing Uncle Mac gave my Mom time to think about his heavy request. At first blush, she was sceptical because the thought had never crossed her mind to give up any of her beloved children. Her life as a single parent entailed working long hours, which included lots of overtime just to make ends meet and somehow, she managed. As kids, we had everything we needed and knew we were loved because she selflessly put us first above her own needs. She was also very protective of us. Therefore, before making her agonizing decision she discussed it with my grandparents and they were all for it thinking it might help to give her some financial relief.

When my Mom questioned me about how I felt about this life changing request and my initial answer was no. Ultimately, after listening to both of my grandparents, of which my grandmother was Aunt Aretha's sister, tell me all the benefits of staying with my aunt I reticently agreed. The way Nanny and Papa described this huge change was of me essentially being an only child and gaining access to these extra things that ordinarily I would have missed out on.

All the while, my aunt was unaware of the plans my uncle was busily making on her behalf. My Mom still wasn't convinced, yet she feared disappointing my uncle because she loved him and was one of his favorite nieces. She decided she wasn't completely okay with the idea of me moving in full-time, but she would be ok with me going to spend the nights so that she wouldn't be alone. Mom finally gave him an answer. It wasn't exactly what he prayed for, but they both agreed to the arrangement. Uncle Mac was now content and ready to transition knowing that he had everything in order. After everything was in place, he told my aunt about the arrangements he had made with my mom. A few weeks later, he went to heaven.

A BONDING EXPERIENCE

From that point forward, I stayed with my aunt until I became comfortable enough to completely move in. I was ecstatic and comforted by the fact that I could still see my Mom and siblings every day. When school restarted my Mom would drop me off during the weekdays. Then, I spent time in the evening with my brother and sister until it was time to go to Momtee's house.

My aunt and I became close as we grieved the loss of my uncle, her beloved husband. Our shared bond of grieving and healing with each other grew into a loving mother-daughter relationship. I watched as Momtee push through her grief, while I simultaneously worked through my hidden pain of sexual abuse, at the hands of a close neighbour. In the first year with Momtee, I built up the courage to share and bring back into remembrance all the painful encounters I had battled secretly. I begged my Momtee not to tell my mother about the abuse because I was so traumatized.

Under the threat of my abuser telling me that if my Mom ever found out she would kill him and serve time in prison. I feared the thought of my siblings and I growing up without a mom. A secondary fear was that I did not want to live with it being my fault that someone was dead because of me. Fortunately, she honored my request and only told one other adult, my grandmother. They both held on to the secret to protect me. I no longer had to carry the burden of maintaining such a traumatic secret by myself.

Things weren't talked about openly like they are now, so I still had to endure seeing the abuser almost daily because he lived across the street from my grandparent's house. After my Mom's work schedule changed we no longer had to be subjected to him. Thanks be to God; those years of agonizing torment were finally over. Over time, the burden began to lift, and I could be a kid again.

My Momtee taught me everything you could imagine. It was like being on an adventure every day as she introduced me to the world of quilting, picking out fabric, cutting out patterns, sewing, making homemade soap, how to can apple jelly, fresh fruit peach and plum preserves, shelling peas and picking greens. I adored watching her make hot water cornbread, dumplings, gingerbread, homemade pies, fried pies, cakes, and tea cake all from scratch. I can still smell the scent of pure vanilla, ground cinnamon, nutmeg, and fresh cream butter wafting throughout the house. We even washed and hung clothes outside to dry in the wind.

Many of my childhood peers missed out on these special experiences. She desired to teach me in the self-sufficient manner her generation was taught. She also taught me the importance of hospitality and etiquette. On Sundays she would send me to drop off plates to the elderly neighbors in the community, and if someone were ill or bereaved we would make homemade soup and a full course dinner for their family. We ate every meal together, and she took her time listening to me talk about my day. During our special time together in the evenings she would tell me that God has so much more planned for my life. And unlike when my uncle told me, I slowly began to embrace her words in my spirit.

The most miraculous thing happened to me after my uncle died, I discovered a chest of drawers that belonged to him. It contained hand written notes, bibles, books, and all kinds of interesting trinkets. No one else was around so I would take this time to rummage through the drawers for hours, and this daily act lead me to a love of reading, and introduced me to God. In a divine way my uncle was teaching me about God and the habit of having quiet time with him. I learned that our Heavenly Father loves me unconditionally, was my protector, and I could be set free from sadness and fear. I could enjoy life and breath. I could play freely without worry about being touched inappropriately, or enduring painful sex acts that were too much for my innocent child mind to process and handle.

There were times I would watch my aunt pray and cry out to God while on her knees. She would beckon me to her and begin to pray. Through this practice, I developed a personal relationship with God. I would read children's bible stories as she read her bible. Reminiscing about these peace filled moments gives me chills. I no longer feel shame, dirty and nasty from being violated. I feel a sense of freedom, revival, peace, and most of all innocence.

My life with Momtee was not always a rosy story. I had to endure over hearing rumors from people making ugly allegations about my mother presuming she had abandoned me and was a bad parent. None of that was true, but of course other people didn't understand what took place during that time before my uncle died. My older cousins thought I was getting special treatment and what could possibly be so special about me that I was the one chosen for this special life with Momtee. As I got older, individuals continually sewed discord because they assumed I loved Momtee more than my birth mom. I would hear over and over she is not your mom she is just your aunt. Internally this callous dialog would rip me to pieces because she was my mother too and I loved her the same.

Upon graduating high school and college I still could maintain a close relationship with Momtee. Despite people thinking I was only sticking around to gain something from my beloved Momtee, I didn't care. I knew the truth of our relationship and she did too. I love her with all my heart and I understand that God has somehow blessed me with two special mothers to love and have them love me. It has been a challenging road trying to prove my love to one and not slight the other.

I still talk to Momtee every day before and after work. Sometimes, in the middle of the day I would call her and ask her to pray for my patients or to just talk to me when I was having one of those days. I talked to her about absolutely everything and still do. We have no secrets as I have shared things with her that good, bad and ugly and she has loved me the same. Another reason I love her so dearly is she prays daily for me and one of her favorite sayings is "Do unto others as you want to be treated and I pray that God would have you be all that He wants you to be."

MY LOVE STORY TODAY

Today, I am beyond proud to be blessed to have two mothers in my biological Mom Deborah and my loving Aunt Aretha. My mom still feels left out sometimes, but she loves me so much that she chooses to understand and accept our bond. My aunt is my Momtee, simply put she is my mother. I love her dearly and there is nothing in this world that could ever compare to the love we share. It doesn't matter that I was never connected to her through an umbilical cord or breastfed, what matters to me is the love she has shown me unconditionally. She loves me despite my flaws and celebrates me when I am up. I love her spirit, joy, laughter, nurturing, and the woman that can pray the house down. She will forever be my mother and will always live within my heart. Right now, I am taking care of her, as she is fighting to stay here on earth. As each day passes I dread what life will be like without her. I have been here every step of the way since my uncle passed and don't want to miss out on any time with her. I cherish every part of her and every lesson I was blessed to learn. She will always remain in my heart forever as my mother because I have learned that loving two mothers is not only possible, but beautiful.

WHAT I HAVE LEARNED

I would like to encourage anyone who has a strong desire to be a mother, but hasn't been able to have children. I would encourage you to find one child or several children and make a huge impact on their lives. You would be surprised how much you will impact them daily. Many children are just looking for someone to listen to them and give them the attention they need. Motherhood comes in many forms, and non-traditional motherhood is just as meaningful because you choose to be the parent of that child. Don't be afraid to adopt, there are millions of children seeking loving homes and loving mothers to guide and nurture them. There are so many options instead of full-time commitment, volunteer, mentor, become a foster parent or a child advocate. I want to encourage women who have not experienced what it's like to have a loving mother to ask God to send someone in your life that will take on that role. You are never too old to be loved unconditionally. Finally, remember family is not solely based on DNA. Family is based on unconditional love, commitment, and support. Most importantly, love each other unconditionally. Know that love is one of the greatest gifts that God has given us on earth and it is powerful beyond measure.

ABOUT THE AUTHOR

Kimberly Armstrong resides in the USA. She is an advocate, survivor, inspirational speaker, and finds writing therapeutic. She enjoys empowering others to find their voice bringing them hope and healing. Inspired by her own life experiences she advocates for the voiceless. She promotes awareness of all forms of sexual abuse, sex trafficking, domestic violence, and religious manipulation. Her aim emphasizes the importance of mental health to overcome, thrive, and speak out loud. By passionately giving back to the community through volunteerism and community service has proven to give her life beyond measure including surviving cancer. Kimberly enjoys hosting empowerment classes, equipping the community with signs to look for and how to help those that are trying to find their voice. Kimberly is determined to knock out shame, guilt, and unworthiness, with lots of love in a judgement free environment. She is now accepting invitations for speaking engagements, panels, and classes.

CONTACT

Email: KimArmstr@gmail.com

LOVE UNBOXED: AN ANTHOLOGY BY WOMEN FOR WOMEN

PART THREE

PATIENCE, SURVIVAL AND BROKEN DREAMS

THE FORGOTTEN HEARTBEAT
Debra Gardner: United Kingdom

I could follow the crowd and go no further or walk alone and go places no one has gone before

~ Albert Einstein

BABY STEPS

Marilyn's life journey starts at the tender age of 11 months old, living in a children's home in the south of the United Kingdom, the only comfort a small black squeaky doll with a cute pony tail. Leading up to the abandonment her mother Nika aged 19 beautiful and shy arrived at Southampton docks in the south of England by boat 'The Boguna', leaving behind a very poor and humble life in the Caribbean. Travelling for a minimum of six weeks this proved to be an emotional and tiring boat journey. She was accompanied by one of her six siblings Lockie the younger brother, Nika's dream was to finally settle in the United Kingdom close to her younger sister Gina, mother and father.

Two years later, Nika aged 21 was a young mother to baby Marilyn, life was proving difficult, especially trying to hold down a full-time job, it didn't help, with all three including her younger brother Lockie, struggling to live in a very small room in a shared house, the bathroom located in the back garden, very little money for rent, bills, food and the costs of day to day living. This poor lifestyle became extremely difficult, especially raising a baby, she started searching for larger and much more comfortable accommodation. Nika asked her sister Gina to take care of baby Marilyn now four months old, until she was settled and in a more practical and easier position.

However, Gina, despite her more confident personality and strength was already leading a difficult and volatile life raising her own six young children and couldn't quite cope, so decided it wasn't possible, not even for a short period. Reluctantly, with no choice Nika asked Peggy, a work colleague and friend who she met whilst working as a machinist in the local clothing factory, to accommodate and take good care of her baby just for a short period whilst trying to get her life together. Unfortunately, because of Peggy's unstable state of mind and mental problems, she had great difficulty coping with a new born and made a personal decision without informing Nika, to hand baby Marilyn over to Social Services.

Without any hesitation, Social Services immediately removed Marilyn from Peggy's home. Marilyn's dishevelled and neglected appearance alarmed the officials and realising the baby was vocally very quiet and hadn't cried, together with the absence of her mother their decision was made. Sadly, after several months of little communication from Nika despite the occasional contact she made with the children's home where Marilyn was now living, it wasn't enough. With no support from family and very little money, she couldn't afford social fees or more importantly the outstanding debt, she made the heart-breaking decision to completely hand her baby over to Social Services in the hope of being reunited with Marilyn in a few months once she was finally settled.

Unfortunately, that day never came, and the reality was to leave the social workers to place Marilyn with a foster family in the hope of a better life, home and future. Nika's last contact with Social Services was to request a photograph of Marilyn, she asked a staff member to file a personal letter and give to Marilyn at the end of her legal fostering age of 18. Nika did manage to visit the children's home just the once with a man, or you could say an old school and childhood friend from her home town in Jamaica. But on arrival she was informed by the officials that until she could prove that her life had positively changed and was stable, it would most definitely be the end of any contact with baby Marilyn, not only for that day but for the rest of her life.

Marilyn's difficult life continued, and at 9 months old she was placed in a Barnardo's home. After a few months, she was photographed and advertised in the local newspaper as a "coloured baby in need of a home" she was finally removed from the children's home and fostered by a Caucasian English family. This new life and environment took her on a long path of heartbreak, loneliness, trauma, racism and insecurity, but thank goodness God blessed her with inner strength and a strong determination to get through this complicated emotional journey. Social Services were ignorant and blasé of the care of babies and young children who had been placed with families of a different culture and background.

Some of Marilyn's new family members and school officials were not in agreement and despised the thought of a child of colour around their environment, which led to bullying and at times horrendous abuse. But there is a blessing, for although Marilyn was placed and raised as the only ethnic child in the new family amongst another fostered brother and adopted sister Elizabeth, the other youngest brother being the foster parents only blood son, strangely from a very young age as siblings the children blended together despite all being homed from completely different cultures, backgrounds and different birth parents they had this underlying strength, protectiveness, love and support for each other, acknowledging that all having been abused, neglected and bullied, which would haunt them for the rest of their lives, they accepted that life ahead was going to be traumatic, but at times their personal laughter and proactive communication would keep them close and strong forever.

A MOTHER'S PAIN AND SECRETS

Nika continued with a new life in the North of England located close to her parents, living with her six birth children and husband, the very same man that two years previously was supportive enough to drive Nika to visit Marilyn in the children's home, then made the awful decision to return home 150 miles to the North of England without her baby. Nika's life, although surrounded by family was at times deeply sad and depressing, one of the reasons for sure being the emptiness of abandoning her daughter. She often spoke about what happened to her first born with her other six children, about Marilyn their half-sister, and she displayed a framed photograph of Marilyn as a baby in the kitchen on view for everyone to see. She had no idea of the abusive environment in which she had left her innocent child and she continued with her day to day life, raising her family and working locally to her home. Her husband had no idea over the years that she secretly continued to write letters to the Social Services officials, desperate to know about her little girl almost begging for photos and news.

In the meantime, to conceal her pain and heartache, she spent social time smoking, drinking and gambling with her father and when possible visiting her sister Gina in London. Although not a close relationship, they found comfort in each other especially after losing their brother Lockie age 40 from a heart condition, who she travelled with from the Caribbean. Another brother also passed away with a similar heart condition at a similar age, leaving her and sister Gina, another brother and parents. Shamefully, Nika's parents and the other elders had no intention of trying to persuade the husband to reconsider bringing Nika's baby home. In fact, they were too racist, although of colour themselves and of Indian descent, Marilyn half Indian darker skinned and unknown father didn't stand a chance of fitting into this blood family, therefore abandoned and left in foster care, whatever the condition it didn't matter, she didn't matter, both families blood or not didn't care!

THE LOST SCENT

Forty years have passed, travelling 150 miles from London to the North of England Marilyn sits looking up at the sun, deep in thought speaking to her mother who she sadly never touched, spoke nor shared this precious life with, not even knowing her scent, but holding a heartfelt letter. She carried a beautiful bouquet of sunflowers delicately wrapped ready to leave on her mother's gravestone, in her prayers thanking God and speaking of eternal gratitude to be finally home to her beloved birth mum, finally at peace in both hearts. The emptiness will always remain of not meeting her mother, living all those years not knowing where she came from or her identity, the pain and emptiness almost heeled, but never for one moment forgotten.

THE JOURNEY

Marilyn's deep sadness came from knowing that her mother died very young aged 39, leaving behind 7 children. She died from a stroke and heart failure, the after effects of the stroke leaving Nika's beautiful face deformed. She suffered from depression and drinking, her precious young life ended very abruptly in hospital. At times her words to the other children even from her hospital bed, "we must travel and find your sister Marilyn", sadly that day never came and the pain for both Nika and Marilyn of not meeting each other will never leave their hearts, but the true light and happiness of finding her mother's final place of rest is a treasured blessing, although both grandparents are buried just two rows behind her mother's headstone, it brings darkness and anger knowing they contributed, and were helped by the others to abandon her as if she never existed.

The long emotional journey for Marilyn tracing her birth mother was extremely difficult, never giving up and searching through various channels, she managed to trace the family history through an international online tracing website with the support of her loving sister Elizabeth. Although this was a difficult and almost an impossible search, this was due to Marilyn being given the wrongful information at the age of 18 by Social Services, this was recorded on her birth certificate, her registered mother was Mexican not Jamaican, father unknown and it showed an incorrect date of birth, which meant that she had unknowingly been celebrating an incorrect birthday, living a life of false identity and only realising her true identity some 40 years later. The surname and nationality were not only incorrect, but she was also shocked to discover whilst sat at the cemetery sadly reading her mother's headstone that the date and month of her birth were identical to her mother, 29th June. Social Services had no thought or care the impact it would have registering the false information about the future of Marilyn not knowing her identity and correct date of birth.

Looking back Marilyn will never forget the day she plucked up the courage and followed the trail from the information logged with the online ancestry search website, waking up in the morning taking a shower deciding what to wear whilst full of anxiety, not knowing what's ahead, is she going to find her mother? at this address, if not where?

So off she set on her journey to the North of England, in her hand the letter that her mother Nika left on file with Social Services ready for the time she reached the end of the legal fostering age of 18. The sad content of the letter was heart breaking, Nika begging Social Services to visit her daughter whilst in the children's home or at least to see a photograph. Cruelly, the officials adamantly closed the doors and that day never came, but for Marilyn to treasure this old, discoloured and beloved letter in her mother's hand writing was the magnet and sign that she was never going to give up searching for her mother, not ever!

Three hours later, knocking on a neighbour's door in a small-town North of England an elderly couple confirmed their neighbour of many years was indeed living in the family house. So, Marilyn stepped over the wall and nervously rang the doorbell, she could hear someone walking towards the door, every step timed with every heart beat until finally the door opened. There stood, glaring, an old miserable hard-faced white English woman with dirt and mud smeared over the front of her white t-shirt and white jeans, thick gold cheap jewellery hanging around her neck also covered with grime.

Marilyn explained the delicate story of searching for her mother and not knowing who she was, the only concrete truth she was the daughter of Nika, asked humbly if she could see her mother. The woman, with a huge smirk and appearing angered, harshly replied "of course you know who you are look at the colour of your skin black isn't it" and nastily persisted "no you can't, your mother died, she's buried down the road at the local cemetery, in fact I've just left the graveyard cleaning the headstone". At that moment, Marilyn had fallen to the ground breathless, heartbroken, and devastated with uncontrollable tears.

The hard-faced woman, still holding the door open, turned her head and bellowed down the hallway to that same man, Nika's widowed husband, "you have a visitor, Nika's daughter so she said? do you want to see her," his cold response "not at the moment I'm sleeping". Marilyn picked herself up off the ground, turned away from the door, weak but with pride, completely traumatised, with only a mobile number handed to her.

That same widowed man, 6 blood siblings, Uncle Pato, Aunty Gina, and other family members, have never made any attempt to search and locate their half-sister Marilyn, the daughter their mother always loved to her dying day. The strained relationships with the blood siblings and family are just another complicated sad story. Just before leaving her late mother's home, driving back down the motorway later that same day, the sullen woman gave Marilyn the phone number and address of her Uncle Pato, after another emotional meeting, he gave a lifetime of information and the address of Aunty Gina, who shockingly lived 25 minutes from Marilyn's home in London and an unbelievable 15 minutes from her office. She was later to find out that Gina was the sister who turned her own sister Nika and baby Marilyn away. But with strength and persistence the aunt was a way of Marilyn getting to know her mother and family history, it was the one and only opportunity to know the truth? She thought?

Secrets and lies were untold, the aunt passing away couple of years on. Marilyn will never know the truth and whereabouts of her birth father and not all the truth about the family. When Nika was 21 years old,

Marilyn's father visited her at Gina's house in fact he named Marilyn. Keeping communication channels open, when he returned to America he posted personal letters to Gina's house for Nika in the hope that both Nika and their daughter would join him for a new life, but somehow Nika never received any letters due to someone intercepting Post, which lead to the long distant relationship sadly ending.

Marilyn was raised from a lower-class background, through the harshness of her life she had inherited and gained inner strength to keep focused, positive, strong, fiercely independent and a drive of life and ambition that you can only gain and maintain with life experiences. With trauma and disappointments, you have two choices: sink or swim. Marilyn knew that her mother battled with life and the unbearable loss of her first-born child never healed, she was also aware her foster brothers and sisters battled through their childhood within and outside the family home, therefore Marilyn had a duty to survive and remain strong. Although ridiculously hard at times, life nearly got the better of her, but her mother's spirit gave her strength to stay on the path of success and to love herself regardless, the decision not to let anyone or any situation, no matter how painful, ever take her spirit.

Growing strong and getting used to this life, Marilyn proudly entered the world of modelling and became a professional model. This opened many doors including TV, fashion, photographic assignments, commercials, and advertising campaigns. The career offered fantastic opportunities gave her the confidence to travel the world and meet interesting people.

Ten years in the modelling and film business, with life experiences, she knew it was not a career to maintain forever, so she made a huge decision to hang up a little of the glamour and become a successful business woman, entrepreneur, she set up her own international multilingual staffing and recruitment agency. The agency provides brand Ambassadors, corporate and hospitality staff, supervisors and event managers and continues to work with high profile clients. Marylyn travels the world working with the various clients, from the Grand Prix in Monaco, International Motor Shows, worldwide sporting events in the United States, the World Cup Rio de Janeiro Brazil, the Olympics and Para Olympics in the United Kingdom to the amazing charity events for Ronald McDonald, Barnardo's and many more.

Setting up a company to support and employ staff has its personal satisfaction, motivating a happy team and every day working at maintaining a successful business is priceless. She hopes this reflects and provides a sense of inspiration to those who may also have had a similar background, or even those who just feel insecure and rejected in life. Marilyn's leadership knowledge, purely gained through leading her own life, perhaps didn't always get it right, but it's the only way to learn. Above all, finding love and true emotional connection has been a long journey of trust, something she still working on, God willing, now on the right path paved ahead, her soul at peace, finally time to acknowledge trust and love.

CONCLUSION

Debra will continue to share her personal true-life stories and hopes this message will help those who are too reserved, anxious or insecure to speak out, which will enable them to live life to the fullest. To cope with adversity and overcome hardship, abuse and heartache and succeed to accomplish whatever is in your heart and mind, be patient with yourself, don't let the severity of any negativity cast a long shadow over your precious life, channel that passion to energy, you have to turn from a victim to a victor. Live your dreams and never give up hope!

ABOUT THE AUTHOR

Debra Gardner born in England.

Left school as a teenager enrolled with Rolls Royce Aerospace as a trainee, gained secretarial experience to become a full-time employee. Left Rolls Royce to register self-employed thereafter worked as a full-time professional model in the United Kingdom, America, Dubai, Europe and South Africa, involved in various TV commercials and films at Pinewood and Elstree Studios.

Whilst modelling, attended and thoroughly enjoyed drama school located Islington London.

A successful entrepreneur setup a successful business. DGP International Agency provides professional multilingual staff for corporate hospitality, Conferences, weddings, and charity events, working in the United Kingdom America, Brazil, Dubai, Monaco and Europe.

Inspired and donates to deserving children's charities and animal trusts

After a traumatic childhood, she has a passion and a goal to help and mentor those with a similar background and guide them to a journey of abundance of success and happiness.

CONTACT

Website: www.dg-promotions.co.uk
Email: debrag5@hotmail.com

SAY A LITTLE PRAYER
Mary Martin London: United Kingdom

Dedication is the best way to success. Believe in yourself

~ Mary Martin London

GOING IT ALONE

I just stepped off the catwalk at the African Fashion Week, at Freemasons hall in August 2017. Being the headlining act (Mary Martin London,) took me right back to my childhood. Yes!! this is where it begins.

I grew up in the 60s. My parents, were Ministers. My Beautiful mother {Cynthia} was Jewish/Jamaican and my father{Eric} was a Ghanaian born in Jamaica. Together, we were a family of 13 and of course I, was the middle child, in a line of seven brothers and sisters, who called me, 'Mary with the seven devils'. I was a troubled child, a loner, (I would say) as my parents only took notice of the elders and youngers. I was forgotten, specially as I was a flamboyant child, always loved wanting to be the centre of attraction.

It wasn't long before I was put in a children's home {in the 70s John Cane, Dr Bernardo's] I was also a 'troubled and lost child' because my brothers and sisters would keep saying "Here comes Mary with the seven devils". I never could understand why they treated me this way.

I remember it clearly that bright sunny day, driving from Cardiff out into the Welsh Valleys! I remember I hated crossing the Seven Bridge. My fear of falling off that bridge to my death was real! I was in my father's church mini bus, with all my brothers and sisters piled in to see me off. They dropped me in the grounds of a big house, similar to the Harry Potters house. I looked up and it was very scary for me, when I turned around to witness my brothers and sisters waving, as they drove off leaving me there standing! I will never forget that day.

I looked up to the sky and said *"lord! you are the only other father I know! will you be my father?"* I guess he answered "Yes" Ever since that day, I walked with God.

I was a wayward child; getting pregnant at the age of 14! Not good... It was the first time, I had ever done anything like that, it just happened! Funny thing though! I did not realise until four weeks to the birth I was even pregnant. How naïve can one be! It just goes to show, that children really need (real) parental guidance. When my daughter Celetia was born, it was hard for me as I was still a child myself! However, I always trusted in God, who sent me an angel by the name of Carol Hudson. She has been my life-long friend, to this day and (I would say) a segregate mother to my kids loll! She might as well be, as she cared for my daughter for a very long time. I am eternally grateful to her and her husband Patrick, they have been a blessing to me.

I used to get in a lot of trouble while growing up because I was totally ignorant and never listened to anyone (not even my parents). I had not gone to school (always being in and out of the children's homes) I did not know any different. Even though I was very smart and intelligent, I was ignorant and hard of hearing at the same time. It's a long story, so we will skip that bit and get straight to the point.

I sought education for myself later on in my life and still cannot believe that I did that! I was frightened to tell anyone that I could not read or write and was ashamed, so I kept bluffing my way, or I would ask my friends to write for me or my boyfriends to read to me. It went on and on throughout most of my life in this way.

On several occasions, I would book myself on courses to learn how to read and write but always felt embarrassed, (being the eldest in the class) so I would always give up. Somehow, the thoughts of my lack of education, kept returning back to me at several different stages of in life, the 80s and 90s but the year 2000 was the final straw.

I had been married to a very possessive man. Yes, I married [a Muslim} and was not allowed out at all. He was very strict with me and being a Christian, I did not know the difference with the religions, as I thought people were all the same. Boy! Did I get that all wrong! Once again, another wrong choice in my life, only this time, I was stuck with it... as I had married him. It was a very bad and abusive relationship at this point in my life, so bad that I suffered in silence, not knowing who to turn to, or were to go. I was not allowed to have my friends or family around either, so he overtook my life like an infection. I was at a dead-end road, no left nor no right turning for me; just a big full stop.

THE BIG FIGHT BACK

This relationship lasted 16 years, with eight years in love and eight years out of love, trying to get away. However, eight years into the relationship he got very ill. I went to the doctors with him, for a diagnosis. As he spoke to the doctor, I glanced over at his doctor's notes facing me upright on the desk, barely able to read them. I could not believe it! My heart gasped with fright and fear, as I read in the notes, that he had been a patient in a mental institution {Maudsley Mental Hospital} from the age of 14.

To my surprise, the day I had met him, was the day he was released... God knows I tried! I quickly got my composure and thoughts. I remembered. 'Oh my God!' If you noticed, throughout my journey within my marriage, God was not mentioned. I was so use to calling him before... I had been in this awful marriage but now knew the truth about his violence and abuse; what was I going to do about it?

Pray, yes! So, I cried. *"lord, I am sorry I had forgotten you for many years. I am so ashamed to call on you now, as I was having a bad time with the new husband I had married and every time I mentioned you father, he cursed your name. It was so painful for me to hear him abuse you, as you are my father. You know, the only way I could live with this man, was to not call your name as he got so angry, so I took all the abuse myself. You know that I found out I was living with a narcissi demon."* I cried again. *"Lord I feel ashamed that I had forgotten you and now things have got so bad lord. Could you ever forgive me? I will understand if you don't lord."* That night I closed my eyes and I had the best sleep ever because I knew my father never left me, he was there with me and it was I, who had left him.

By this time, I just wanted *out* more so now, that I had seen his medical notes. The puzzles in my head were slowly being put together. The reason for him smashing up my car and house, smashing my TV while I was watching it and ripping up all my short clothes and low-neck tops. This guy was a living nutcase, that I would not wish on my worst enemy!

I started to get counselling but it did not seem to help me much, so I prayed and continued with my hard prayers, for all the years I did not pray. I said *"father this man will never leave me, he keeps begging me to let him stay. The only way I will get rid of him lord, is if you send him to another country far, far away."* I prayed the same prayer for weeks and low-and-behold, my father answered me.

Yes, Yes, Yes! God is so good!! My husband, was offered a job in America and asked me if he should take it. I said *"Yes"* without hesitation (my heart pounded fast) knowing that my father would never forsake me. Just the thought of him (my husband) leaving me, was so exciting. Within one month, he asked me again if I was sure that I didn't want him to stay. I said "No, it's the best move you could ever make". He then packed up and left. The taxi came, and I watched him drive slowly away. It felt so good, with no more looking over my shoulder to experience him stalking me. I was free, I WAS FREE!!

MAKING THE RIGHT CHOICES

What am I going to do? Where am I going to with my life? Yes, I am truly stuck in a time warp. My life had ended when I met my husband and all my values in life, my compassion and everything else had gone. I was an empty shell now, not knowing what I was going to do next.

First thing I told myself was to pray, my father was there waiting and wanting me back in his fold". Amen!

Again, I asked *"Lord help me, help me Lord. I know I have been asking you for a lot of things lately but, would it be possible for you to give me back the talent that you gave me as a child, the one you blessed me with from birth. I promise to use it to the best of my ability".*

Low and behold, God blessed me with the hands I

have again today and gave me the inspiration, the love and the ability to create, so this is what I did. I took a break for six months to get focused Carol Hudson [my good friend] helped me back on my feet. *I just love her and her husband Patrick; I am forever in their dept.*

I went to study. Yes, I was embarrassed, but the devil was not letting me leave this time! I wanted to learn, so I went back stronger wearing Gods armour. I stayed and studied hard at the course and finally passed both my GCSE English and Maths with A's. I then started to design and construct my own clothes. Things were looking good. My friends would come and purchase my designs and my life was changing.

I said {in 2014] to myself 'let me go and study fashion at the London college of contemporary arts LCCA' [when I was younger, I had two scholarships, to go to London school of fashion but I never turned up. I could not read or write at that time.] However, I recently did a HND and finally Graduated at the LCCA. The Dean Sagi, called me out at the graduation and stated that the college was proud to have Mary Martin, as a rare and special student that did not appear often at its establishment. In short, there was no pupil like me.

I was so proud of myself! I had broken down the fear of self-doubt and not wanting to learn! Well!! I always believed I was never good enough before, with that self-doubt, always there like a thorn in my head. I did finally believe I was strong enough. Yes! I previously thought, that doubt only set in, when I left my father and the Devil tried to stop me receiving my blessing,

I HAVE ARRIVED

To date 2017:

I receive an international Achievers award for Best Female Designer, in November 2014 (BEFFTA) and honoured for fashion inspiration. Also in June 2015 honoured for the Best African Designer by Mercedes Benz. I am delighted to say that at last, that I have made the right decisions. *Sometimes we pick a wrong road but are destined for change.*

It took me all my life, to understand but I finally got there! Life truly began very late for me but I want to be an inspiration to other women that have encountered bad life experiences whether through a relationship, or through fear of that change.

I am here, just to let you know, that its ok! Life is what you make it! I have made some good new friends and lost a few along the way but I have never ever completely left my father. You too can make that change! Who would have ever thought that this young lady Mary (with the seven devils) would turn out to be Mary with the seven Angels.

He has never forsaken me. Without him, I would never have made it.

MY LIFE TODAY

Today I am making progress. I am studying at UEL {East London university} for my degree! It has been a long journey, but I have reached destination's door and I feel fuller. All my trials, have made me the person I am today. I would never look back on the bad times; I just want to enjoy the good times. Like I said: *life is what you make it! Never give up on your dreams; only the strong survive!*

I am finally going to get the papers. A DEGREE!!

Thanks to my special father!

SHEEP IN WOLVES CLOTHING

Sometimes in life, we think friends are there to protect us when really, they are there to block us. Many times, in my life I came to that dead-end road no one was there. The people I thought were friends, were my enemies trying to stop my success. {I call them the devils angels} Jealousy is a very bad spirit, that can make a person so envious, that they do things you would never expect them to do. It's like a virus, that grows and grows. I have always had a discerning spirit that gave my friends a lot of chances. Nowadays, my fabric is my first love and my friends! After all, I still have my special father that guides me all the way.

ABOUT THE AUTHOR

The very talented, dynamic and inspirational award-winning fashion designer, Mary Martin London enjoyed a successful career in the music industry early on, but developed a keen interest in fashion over the years. Today, Mary Martin London is recognized as one of the leading international fashion designers and very much respected by her peers around the world. Mary Martin London is known for her fabulous, bespoke, creative designs that not only breaks the rules but makes the rules; Mary has an impressive celebrity clientele that are always vying for a classic signature red carpet show piece that demands the world's attention, every time.

Mary Martin London's collections include a tribute to the late "David Bowie", the "Cecil the Lion Dress" that went viral and was featured on the BBC News. In numerous editorials including The Huffington Post, The Daily Mirror, The Telegraph, Elle, French magazine 'Slave', magazine Or

CONTACT

Website: www.marymartinlondon.com
Email: ilmood@hotmail.com

AN INTIMATE PASSAGE TO NEW-NESS
Queen Irena: United Kingdom

There is a tiny voice within me saying "Believe and I will be with you". Solace enough for me!
Love Is a Spider's Web By

~ Queen Irena

WORKING ON THE REMNANTS

Wearing my usual invisible mask, while I held onto my walking stick to make the short journey up the road from the car to the gym building was not easy at all. In-fact it was like climbing the highest mountain! Who was I kidding back then though! I struggled with each step, leaning hard on what was my support, feeling much pain right through me, was all I had by way of hope at that time. Not surprising for someone so visually obese and disabled to onlookers. In fact, I was more than 23 stones (146kg) back then, with hypotension, hypo-cholesterol and arthritis. I was also fighting with remnants from a lifetime of sexual and emotional abuse, which had certainly got my 'knickers in a twist' and had me eating all variety of foods and sweets to comfort me. I aimed to fill the holes in my soul with all the stuff I ate, since no-one else could. Instead, I finally began to realise that I would only grow fatter and unwell enough to unwittingly commit suicide with my 'death by eating misadventures'.

The memories of my children helping me out of the sitting room chair, or thoughts of them struggling to carry my casket at my funeral, or the shame for them being told that my death was due to my overeating, was far too much for me to contemplate the impact it would have on them. I had previously cried and prayed for years throughout loosing earlier babies to miscarriages and stillbirths, to now go on and cause them the pain of watching me suffer in this way within this predicament was unthinkable. My whispered prayers continued 'Oh, Jah help me to find my way through this difficult life'.

Even with all the wanting of a better life; doing something about it was an incredible task too. The enormous issues in my life took me in and out of various negative and positive realms, that I could not fully express verbally. With constant reminders of my responsibilities, I was forced to act and put things right in my life, to redress the stress being faced by my children. I qualified as a gym instructor, to motivate myself into the tasks that would help my son through his own emotional breakdown by working out with him on small apparatus we had at home. This worked wonders for him, but only a short while for me because of the physical pain and sheer energy it took to keep going with everything and by the pursuit of social services to break me down, for being 'articulate while on state benefit'. However, following a failed attempt to build a business (well not failed, I just had to close everything down to better deal with my family matters in its place), the focus was off my path to New-Ness and back on everyone else again. If I could have run like a sprinter at that time, I think I would still be running like Forest Gump, to this day!

QUEEN BY EXPERIENCE

To those on the outside, I was like superwoman in many ways. A mother of seven, who had the knowhow regarding what was needed to put the world to rights. I possessed specialist skills that dealt with difficult people (including some of my children) and all manner of parenting crisis situations, that everyone else would run a mile from. There were always issues that surfaced in my life that floated around matters of abuse and victimisation that I also had coping mechanisms for. I was even brave enough to take on study for two degrees while the children were very young too. This made me finally awaken to the realities of my complex life by some of the other students that became very distressed about what (I felt) were trivial matters, which I would simply chew and spit out. Somehow, the mention of areas in my life that I found slightly annoying was like a recipe for a breakdown for some in my cohort at university. So much so, that I stopped my occasional comments about my life because the minor reflections of my daily chores seemed too much for them to bear.

I became very protective of myself from reactions I would receive in general regarding my family life, so I held back on my own freedom to speak out my pain, replacing it with outside professional support instead. Some were helpful, others were more work for me than those that claimed to be professionals.

I used all the therapies under the sun to assist me through my difficulties. Some professionals were unable to deal with the issues I had, so I was never able to talk about them as deeply as I needed to. The thing about dealing with mental health professionals is they have this misconception that someone experiencing major life events that remain in one piece, mess up their generic criteria and sometimes highlight their own mental disorders. By not having a non-judgmental coaching approach to issues presented to them, we lose great people to mental institutions.

I remember seeing a psychologist and explaining my solution to a fight my two children (on the autistic spectrum) had and how I felt upset about having to hide my anger from them at the time. Now instead of praising me for how I handled things, the fool telephoned social services, to tell them there was a violent attack on my then seventeen-year-old, by his older brother. Now I was left to explain this to my family who became distressed and of course, one became suicidal at the possibility of the family being split if the services became involved. It's a good thing, I am anointed with the ability to educate some professionals (working in safeguarding posts to protect vulnerable young adults) regarding the behaviour of those on the autistic spectrum. How I dealt with the added burden of one of mine, now on suicide watch, was way out of their league.

Look Man! I had been running things in my home with my children alone and orchestrating all manner of fun activities for them, the community and for my brother with mental health issues, as well as supporting local projects with funding bid writing, training management committee members, writing project proposals, contracts, running workshops, giving advice and information and so much more. There were many individuals scrambling to use me to sort out their lives and ideas and it was (at times) wonderful to be appreciated for my skills; yet also damaging to me in other ways. The ones that took advantage of my need to utilise my knowledge outside mothering, know who they are (there were so many) I forgive them and continue to send my best wishes, yet also take some responsibility for my need to be needed.

NATURAL GROUNDINGS

Life with my children has continued to be the very best ingredient for my self-esteem though. I can hold my head up and testify that I have done the very best mothering with the skills I was anointed with. I am the first to admit, that I have made mistakes along the way too, shouted and cursed but most of all, I have given the best of my love and provided a mothering foundation that cannot be bought anywhere in the world. All you need to do is ask them and they will tell you the truth, by the impact they now have in the world because of the grounding they have gone through. Mothering my children has taught me important lessons and given me hope for a great future from the love and experiences I have shared and still share with them.

You may be wondering when I would mention the father of my children. Well, we got married in Jamaica, when I was twenty-seven. My first son (fathered by another) was nearly eight months old (so many stories to write about). I took on his two children aged six and four and we went on to have four more children together and lived happily here in London. No that is too simple!

So, after a long line of various abusive experiences and my recurring illness within my marriage to him, I put an end to our time together. I suppose I could have killed him off but before I had the chance, he left me alone with the children without physical, emotional or financial support. Somehow, this event was just the beginning of my healing process. I was given the opportunity to start a life without the burden of pretending I was happy around him whenever the children would witness us together. That was hard work! I could finally sleep freely now, without awaking to that terrible pain, only to find that it was because my bladder was full, and he was sexing me during my sleep. Real nasty, messed up stuff, that some would recognise as part of their recurring nightmare! I now had freedom from an unclean man on top of me in the early hours, replaced by quality time with the children, to laugh and play with like normal beings without his manipulating vibrations around us.

I managed to document spontaneous snippets of my life events in my published book 'Love Is a Spider's Web' back in 2003 (I'm in the process of re-launching it in the new year too) which helped thousands to heal though their pain, yet still, this was not enough for me to be alright! My children needed me to fight the daily battles they faced from the pain of life without their father wishing to see them, or supporting me to give them life lessons to learn from. I had to fight off the catalogue of issues, that the racist world outside had in store for their beautiful black selves too. Writing certainly helped me to have an outlet at least.

There were various times when I continued to over-eat, with the thought of the enormous task ahead of me. Don't get me wrong, change of lifestyle is no flipping joke! It is so massive, I had to go away many times alone just to be in my own company, so that I could face my own thoughts, cries and screams. During my travels throughout Jamaica, Florida, Gambia, Canada, Belgium, and Grenada I threw myself on a bed and curled myself into a ball and rocked like a baby before I could see myself for who I really am and begin to take serious action toward my repair. So, don't laugh at anyone who you regard as fat, ugly, over loud, or quiet. In fact, don't laugh at anyone without their permission because you don't know a darn thing about them, or even your own self yet!

My last attempt to opt out of my responsibility for reducing the fat on my body, was to ask for a referral to have gastric bypass surgery. So, there I was, visiting Kings College Hospital and going through assessments for this major operation to change my size and I began to comfort eat again because this made me feel like I had failed myself and I set others to do the work I knew I could do myself. I felt like a complete failure. On the day I was called by the booking clerk with the date (three days later) for the procedure, my mind visualised the carving up of my body on the operating table and I shouted, "I CHANGED MY MIND" and waited for a response. "What" said the Clerk. I repeated "I CHANGED MY MIND!!". Silence, then she announced, "Alright then, I will let your consultant know and he will write to you". This was the real changing moment for me and a chance for my re-birth. I could orchestrate my healing from all the knowledge and skills that I already have and most of all, from the real love I have for myself. I was now ready at last!

RE-BIRTH AND NEW-NESS

Over the last two and a half years, I have put most of my efforts into my complete repair. I cannot say all my efforts because as I said before, I am a mother of a beautiful daughter and six very handsome sons. Knowing that parenthood is forever and more, (OMG! Is it?) you can imagine my workload. Yet still, I have worked hard at repairing my health by working on my mindset, to filter what I subject my hearing to. I work on my ability to filter negative and destructive people out of my life, along with weaning myself off damaging foods and other consumptions that have been detrimental to my health. Yes, I know about the difficulties with the success of this, so I built a fully equipped gym in my house, from gradual purchases at sports shops. Then of course, I used my bid writing skills to gain funding to support my son with his repair through fitness. I gave up my very large bedroom for a much smaller one for our gym, which now have two spin bikes too. It is well used by the whole family but most of all by me, for my health needs and for the health needs of my clients.

I now have a great attitude to health and realise that the limiting belief's that were created within me from all the destructive experiences in my life, were what was killing me. I have learnt that we are constantly targeted to live in fear and pain that cloud the fantastic dream visions, that are awaiting us to reach out and pick up the baton in the relay race to complete happiness.

I have used many methods to renew my health status and have been successful from a much-reduced stress state, therefore my blood pressure returned to normal for a while, although it still is occasionally rather high for various reasons. My arthritis has remained with me, however, due to my exercise routines, my muscles are much stronger, and I am toned, more upright and in control of how my body treats me without medication. The best part of my repair, is that I have (to date) managed to lose 10st 14oz (64kg), through eating a mainly raw, or vegan diet and lightly fried (in coconut oil) delicious vegetables. I can also eat out with friends if I wish, however I tend not to consume after 1 pm but stop by 5 pm. I continue to enjoy my work out sessions on a regular basis and have developed a coaching program that I use to help other serious lifestyle changers (in my home gym) to love themselves, into their own New-Ness. My beautiful people, my continuing stories will empower you to expose your truth too!

ABOUT THE AUTHOR

Queen Irena has an astute way of relating her life experiences that totally empower her readers. An inspirational treasure, Queen glides about her community sprinkling golden love dust on the admirers of her stories; of love and desire, transporting them to a place of self-acceptance. A best-selling author, Queen give's her readers authority, to demand and give unconditional love, to all and will attract you as one of her dedicated readers. Her determination to objectively overcome obstacles from past abusive experiences and from mothering seven children without their father, have empowered Queen to consciously expose her beautiful empathic spirit. She continues to renew her health and build her new business' while coaching individuals and groups into transforming their own lives.

CONTACT

Email: qi@livityweb.com

AT THE END OF THE TUNNEL
Dr Gloria N Harrison: United Kingdom

AUGUST 22ND, 2007, 7.30PM

I do not know how long I stood staring at the tall man with receding hairline. Was he talking to me? His lips seemed to be moving, but I could not hear a word. In my mind he reminded me of a character I saw on TV……. Someone I knew, but was unable to remember.

I looked at him as if in dreamland, was I hearing things? There were people all around speaking to me all at the same time, my mind was buzzing. Doctors and nurses were running around. What were they doing? There was so much noise around me. I could not focus or hear what he was saying, but he was talking to me, at me, there seemed to be panic in the air.

Lord, please wake me up, please. I prayed for the umpteenth time. This must be a dream I am sure. He had no idea what he was saying surely, this is a trance, a joke! Was that sadness I see in his eyes peering out at me through his glasses?

Suddenly, I felt cold hands on my shoulder, shaking me and yet he kept speaking to me.

Now I remember. We were at the hospital for neurosurgery in Enugu.

The next words that came out of his mouth were "I am so sorry doc he has expired".

Time stood still for how long? I don't remember how long.

Can you repeat what you just said Prof? Holding me by the shoulders he repeated "I am so very sorry doc. We did all we could, but your husband passed away at 6.54pm. There was nothing more we could do"

Then the screaming started. But, alas it was true when I saw him on his death bed. He still looked so handsome with his beard, straight nose, dark skin, and robust face.

My husband, my lover, my friend and the father of my five children was dead.

GRIEF

The grieving period did not provide the support or head space I needed. All I remember was the bickering, the gossip, the lies, the unwholesome atmosphere that had become my life and my living.

People mingled in and out of my home as if they owned it or owned my life. I stared at them, I cried a lot back then, and I wished I could die. And, as the burial day approached I succumbed to grief. I became a shadow of myself, not eating; I was not getting out of bed, and work was impossible at this point. Ultimately, I lost about 10kg in total and went from a size 20 to a size 12 for the first month alone.

The succor I had were my family members. My mum and dad, siblings all moved into my home to take care of my young sons who still had no idea what was happening.

For the evening of the wake keeping, I had arranged for a pastor friend to hold the vigil. My colleagues from the hospital where I worked were all around me, my family and friends. My husband's sisters and brothers from the USA and the UK had arrived that day and were all in the house. They avoided eye contact with me and somehow, I knew things did not seem right. These were people I had grown up with in their households and loved for the first twelve years of my life in their family home. I also had all of my kids there. Suddenly I became a stranger and alienated. As the wake keeping progressed and his family was asked to make speeches, all I could remember were his sibling's grief at losing their brother.

Not one of them supported me, or thanked me for taking care of their brother while in hospital. This was when I knew there was trouble ahead.

Even when his father insisted that the burial would be small, with no food or drinks provided for the guests who were to attend as his son died young, my family and friends proceeded to make his burial worthwhile. This was a man who had a family, built a home and had a business. I was not going to bury him like a chicken.

SEPTEMBER 22 ND 2007, THE BURIAL DAY AND ONWARDS

The day started with so much gloom. Faces were frozen from grief.

As was the custom of the Catholic Church to which we belonged, my kids and I chose the white color as our mourning garment. The Hospital had graciously offered free use of the brand-new ambulance to convey the corpse of my late husband.

The procession led from our home to the hospital and to the village where he was laid to rest. There were no dry eyes.

In my grief it was very hard to take in all the events as they progressed. Moving past his corpse was the most difficult and tragic moment of my life. He laid still in his suit and white gloves, still as handsome. His siblings cried, but I was unable to console them as I hurt from what I had heard prior to the day.

Comments were made about knowing who killed their brother and that that person would die within a year of his burial. As the hundreds of people who gathered for the funeral shouted "Ise" I followed suit. I knew they were talking about me in parables, but I kept my cool.

The funeral service in church was another event that I look back on with sadness. I listened to the sermon about death and life and knew that this was the end of my union "Till death do us part".

My third son took the first reading while his brother, my best friend and brother in law took the second reading. After the service, he also came up to the podium and spoke about Leonard and promised to take care of his family, which were myself and my kids.

These were all gimmicks being played out in full glare of the congregation, my friends and my family.

An hour later, the funeral service was over, and the crowd proceeded to the family house for entertainment.

His villager mates refused to place my husband in his grave as they said he was too pompous to join in their village meetings, forgetting that the man lived mostly in the Unites States.

Along came staff of the FMC Umuahia who dug his grave and laid him to rest. Problem solved. This was after they had collected all the tithes due to them. The village setting is an entirely different world sometimes.

Whilst the funeral rites were being concluded, I was taken by several other widows in their village who stripped me down to my birthday suit and proceeded to shave the hair from my armpits, private areas. When it came to my hair, they were stopped by my mother and a barber used his clipper first to take the hair down before they used sharp razor blades to scrape the rest of. After this process, I put my mourning garment back on and just stayed in a corner of the garage, which they had allowed me to use as I was prevented from entering the main house.

I sat and watched my life take a new turn. I was now labelled a widow "nwayi isi mkpe".

There was no sympathy toward me or my situation. I knew most of the sympathisers were there to talk about me and I heard words like "ogboru diya" literally meaning she killed her husband.

My in-laws suddenly had an unusual body language. This Gloria that literally grew up in their household was now an outcast. They would stare at me without saying anything, but I could read their minds. All of them, but only some of them were bold enough to tell me what was being said about me. During the funeral rites, some of his people approached me for money for the drinks supplied from their shop for the funeral. I stared at them and asked what they meant, and they explained that they wanted money to be paid for the drinks since people were bringing money for the bereaved widow. Without delay I asked my mother and sister to count N75,000, as was the balance of the drinks and pay them immediately.

In my heart, I cursed every kobo that was taken away from me for that event.

Funeral over, the night time came to be shouting and fighting upstairs as they quarrelled and argued over money. My mother tried to intervene, but I warned her to stay calm.

We did not sleep that night. It was a troublesome night and my kids all stayed with me on the floor with a mattress as we listened to their ongoing quarrels and what they had to say about me. At this stage, I knew I was truly alone.

AFTER THE FUNERAL, SEPTEMBER 23 RD 2007

As is the custom of the traditional funeral rites an outing service was planned for this day. My late husband's siblings stayed away from me in a different section of the church so as not to contaminate themselves with my children and me. I cried to the Lord in my heart. After the service, his people came to me telling me that there were several traditional rites to follow; one of such rites was staying in the village for a certain number of weeks to continue mourning and a list of other rites I was to observe.

This was followed by a visit from the Umu-Ada of the community to follow up on these rites and what happens next. Unfortunately for them, I had been the President of the Home and Abroad meeting so invariably I was their President.

I humbly informed them that following my in-law's behaviour towards me, I will not be following their traditions. I told them vehemently that now that death had separated us, I would no longer obey them as they demanded. They had shown me hatred at a time I needed them the most. They let me down, let my children down and let their brother down.

After entertaining a few friends who came back for the event, my children and I packed up our luggage into the car, went to my husband's grave side and cried up to the Lord.

I wished him abundant and a restful peace all encompassing. As I knelt by his grave side praying my in-laws were peering at me from the windows making snide comments. Unfortunately for them, I heard them all.

My family and I got into our cars and drove back to Umuahia without a backward glance. Most of the events of this process I have not included in this write up as they were too hurtful.

Ten years ago, was the very last time I have ever saw some of my late husband's siblings. They have never asked about my kids or me and the time that has passed has healed my wounds, but I will never forget them.

LIFE AFTER MY SPOUSE'S DEATH

It was very difficult after the loss of my husband to function.

I suffered from post-traumatic stress and was in a very deep depression. My saving grace was my family who were around me especially my mother.

She was my shield and my anchor when my travails began.

At first, what started as a midnight threat call began the kidnapping saga that I refuse to write about in this story.

Then came the call from various banks to repay the loans my husband had borrowed to fund the business of Atlantic Breeze Ltd, which was into importing heavy duty Mack trucks and various luxury cars and household items. At the time of his death, we had about twenty-five Mack heads waiting at the Port in America to be shipped to Nigeria. I had never travelled to the United States for the entire seventeen years I was with my late husband. That is a story for another day in a world full of deceit.

I had to rely on my in-law to help ship and recover other items, which had been bought so I gave him all the title documents to the trucks. As this is only a summary of events, suffice it to say I never received a penny from the sale of those trucks as he now came up with the story of my late husband was owing him monies, a claim which he could not prove. I lost everything. I had a household to run, children to pay fees for, food, clothing etc. yet I was unable to get any funds from my husband's estate as invariably they were all gone.

The banks Intercontinental bank and Diamond bank were now threatening to sell my home and pay off the loans. As I had no option I sold the land that had been used to store the trucks in Aba and a single truck head, which I found to pay some money to the banks and write to them for time and a payment plan. At this time as well, I started chasing the company Bruckner's Trucks for refunds of some monies they had. They wrote to me to inform me that someone who was my brother in law had come to their offices to say he was my late husband's next of kin without my permission. They then hired lawyers to investigate the case which I paid for. While that was being chased, I started the process of relocation, because of continued threats to my life and spies monitoring both in my workplace and home. I knew my life was now in danger and to protect my kids I had to look for means of skipping the town. I applied to Kings College London for a course and was accepted.

I left the shores of Nigeria in Jan 2009. I left my kids with my mother for her to care for until I found my feet to bring them along.

LONDON, UK

The first few weeks after my Master's degree programme in 2010, I obtained a job and applied to bring my children over to the United Kingdom. They were denied visas at the first attempt and I appealed here in the UK, the presiding judge immediately approved visas for all my kids. This was my first breakthrough. I was offered six months of free CBT by the first-tier tribunal judge for my post-traumatic stress in 2013.

Subsequently in 2013, I proceeded to take the PLAB exams, passed both parts, registered and started practicing as a Mental Health Doctor.

I developed severe hypertension that almost sent me to the grave three times when I suffered suspected heart attacks in 2012/2013 due to stress.

As if this was not enough, after working day and night to pay off my late husband's loan to the banks in 2011, I received a shock that showed someone had come to the bank, connivance with the bank manager at Intercontinental Bank Aba, signed my Certificate of Occupancy and went away with it. This meant my house had been taken away from me. My mother quickly filed to sue the bank and the bank manager for causing emotional turmoil. The case took four years during which time I had petitioned the Commissioner of Police Abia State, EFCC, the Inspector of Police, the intercontinental headquarters in Lagos and reported to everyone I thought could help. The Certificate of Occupancy was subsequently produced back to the Court miraculously by an unknown individual and I won my case against the bank. I sued them for one hundred million naira, but they only paid one hundred thousand naira and offered an apology. At least I had my property back.

The years between 2007 and 2014 were my living nightmares until a day that I would not wish to upon my worst enemies and also would not tell the story in full here.

Today my kids are strapping young men who are slowly healing and realising their full potential. They have grown up to be dependable men who love themselves and are eager to help each other out. My home is full of laughter whenever they are all around.

Most importantly and which I have left for last, I have a new man in my life. He is now the center of my existence and was there for me throughout my trials and tribulations.

We are now married ten years after many late husbands' death and have settled into a beautiful life full of adventures and for that I am most grateful to God.

CONCLUSION

For a long time; I felt pain. I HURT, not because of what faith had heaped upon my life at the tender age of 34 years; but because of the subsequent trauma that my five sons and I had to go through for our survival in a society where material things are valued above human existence.

I tell this story to provide support and hope to women who tragically lost their husbands unexpectedly in an Igbo society.

I tell this story for "WOMEN WITHOUT A VOICE".

This narrative will only be a glimpse into my world as I shall be keeping the rest private.

ABOUT THE AUTHOR

Dr Gloria Ngozi Harrison is a psychiatrist with many years of experience in Mental Health having practiced in both Nigeria and the UK. She is a motivational speaker and a business woman who loves nothing better than giving back to society.

She currently lives in the United Kingdom with her family.

She loves cooking, writing, reading, nature walks, sightseeing and travelling.

CONTACT

Email: GloriaOkorocha2000@yahoo.com

LOVE KEPT ME SANE
Uki Asemota: Nigeria

MY LOVE JOURNEY

I was about 9 years old when, for the very first time in my entire life, I heard that there was a great God. The creator of heaven and earth, He loved me so much that he sent his only begotten son that if I trusted in Him and believed in Him, he would come into my heart and be the Lord of my life. He would direct my affairs and be with me till the end of time. I yearned for that kind of love, especially when I learnt that he would be a father to me.

Do not get me wrong, I had a father. I was the eldest of 5 children but hardly had a relationship with my father. He was a dental surgeon turned business man, who was always away on travels and was hardly home. When he was home, he and my mum were always at each other's throats. There were times when they quarreled, my mother would be sent packing out of the house for several months. This was the kind of family life I grew up in. I can never forget a day when my younger brother saw my parents smiling or talking amicably and he was so, so excited! He rushed in and said gleefully, "Mummy and Daddy are laughing and smiling!" That day and that statement are etched in my memory bank. A day I will never forget.

So for me, I craved love, especially in the family. I craved a father daughter relationship and what a great joy it was when I discovered, after I gave my heart to Jesus, that all that was said about Him was true. I had a personal relationship with him. He was my Father, my friend, my teacher and counselor. He brought perspective to my life and explained to me that man was mortal and full of mistakes and without him the world would keep wallowing in pain and confusion.

I was able to understand my parents and their frailty and kept reaching out to each of them; even my siblings too. I learnt how to pray, study my Bible and lead a life of peace, love and understanding. All through my secondary school, I continually felt His love, presence and guidance. Even throughout university. He, through the person of the Holy Spirit, made me understand that it was not about denomination but a personal relationship with God through his son Jesus Christ. The Bible says [in John 3:16], "For God so loved the world that He gave his only begotten Son, that whoever believes in Him shall not perish but have everlasting Life."

When it came to romantic love, I longed for that man with a heart after God. Someone who loved God above all else, was principled and was someone of integrity. That was the benchmark for me. I ensured throughout my university days that whoever did not fall into this category in my mind I cut off waiting, for that One. My experiences with men will be chronicled in another book. But for this, my Love Unboxed story, I want to share with you how love kept me sane when it looked as though I should have lost my mind.

COULD THIS BE IT?

I graduated from university at the age of 23. Looking to find Mr Right, as I said earlier, I had not had a serious relationship with any man. I guess my standard was pretty high but I still believed in love and the person who would have the same beliefs and passion to serve this God whom I love with all my heart.

I met this young man (well not so young, since when we started dating he was almost 12 years older) as I was about to round up my Youth Service. (This is a compulsory year in Nigeria where you serve the Government.) I loved the fact that he was so organized and disciplined. Yet, when he asked to marry me, I just could not place why, but I knew that this was not the person. But I doubted myself. From all I could see naturally, I had nothing to fear. He was established and was ready to settle down and have a family. But still the nagging feeling would not leave me. It ended after I stayed in that relationship for 10 years. I came to understand that maybe the reasons God was telling my heart that this was not the right person was simply that he was not the person for me.

He might have loved me and I him, but we were not compatible. I do not regret the 10 years in courtship. Well, the story will be in my book. After him, I had one other relationship and that went on for 2 years. After that he broke up with me, saying how he could not continue the relationship. This was someone I had told when he asked me out that I had just came out of 10 years relationship months earlier and I was looking to settling down. He said well, we should give us a try, since he was divorced and wanted to take things slowly. Only to tell me months after we broke up that he thinks he was in love with my younger sister! Someone he had not met personally but was chatting with online through WhatsApp and Facebook.

Ordinarily I should have been bitter, but I still trusted that God had a plan for me and all things work together for good. It is better to be single than to be with someone who might want to have something to do with my sisters or friends. In all this, I knew God still loved me and was planning something ahead for me that I could not understand.

Two years after that relationship ended, God made it possible to get a political appointment, so I had to return to my country after 10 years away. I went back thinking that, just maybe, it was time to believe my prayers for a spouse were about to be answered. I decided to take things slowly. There was a particular man who asked me out and we were just getting to know each other when I got signals that made me uncomfortable. But I remember telling my friend and she told me not to be too hard; I should take my time and just get to know him, etc. On the second date out to chat, he invited me to a motel and I thought this was the second time I was invited to a motel room, so we can chat and all. I remember he locked the door and said he must have sex with me that day. I was a bit perplexed because I was like; we are just getting to know each other and now this? I told him I was not interested in having sex with him and apart from that, I was on my period. After what seemed like an eternity, he took me back home and for the life of me, I can't place why I agreed for him to come to see me again.

I think a few weeks after that he kept insisting on seeing me. I finally agreed, and he came to my office after work hours to visit. I was thinking that that way I would be safe. How wrong I was. He came to my office at about 6pm and we chatted. At about 7pm, or thereabouts, he said he was about to leave and I should give him a hug. That was when everything changed. This person forced himself on me. I have never felt so violated in my entire life. There in my own office, which I THOUGHT WAS MY SAFE SPACE, I WAS RAPED. I kept telling him no, but it seemed as though something else had taken over him.

I remember after he left, I could not scream or anything. I felt shame and anger. But I remember calling that same friend of mine who had advised I should just give him a chance. She was like, go to the nearest clinic and ensure they give you morning after pills and ensure you have all the tests done, etc. I did as she advised but did not request the morning after pills because I am 100 per cent prolife and did not want to do anything against my belief. I never even told the doctor what had happened to me. I think I was sort of ashamed, and also because I led this person into my life. He kept calling me afterwards to plead, saying he was sorry, did not know what came over him but he really liked me, and anytime he was around me he could not help himself. In retrospect, I have come to understand that I always feel I can help change people.

This man was supposed to be a Christian and I felt that we all make mistakes and I ought to forgive him and give him a chance. After all, I was just getting to know him. So about a month after the rape incident, I agreed to see him again and get to know him better. A few weeks into the relationship, I was new in town and my work did not let me socialize much, so we ended up going to my place to chat. And he always forced himself on me. I just could not understand why he behaved like this and the stupid thing about me is I kept praying and saying oh God help him change, and all that.

All this while, in getting to know him, I kept asking if he was married or had children and it was no, he isn't married and no, he does not have children. But anytime I asked to visit where he lived, it was the same oh, I should be patient with him and he would take me to where he lived, etc. I found out I was pregnant, and I cannot forget his first reaction. I was to abort the baby. I told him he was joking. I had never been pregnant in my entire life, never had an abortion and here I was at 38 years of age and you're asking me to end the pregnancy. Even though

I had so many questions and, in a way, felt scared of raising a child all by myself, I was not going to have an abortion. He came over a few days later and said he would support me after all; it was his first child, blah blah blah. I had questions about him. A lot! But now I had a child involved, and all. I can't even remember how I told my siblings about the pregnancy. The most difficult part was telling my boss and my father.

Looking back, I guess I became desperate to settle down. You know that feeling of everyone is married and I need to be settled. I want to have a family and all. I remember when I told my father that my boyfriend wanted to come to see him, as it is customary when the person is asking for your hand in marriage, that my father asked me if my boss had seen him yet. Due to this question and my boss' meeting with him, I found out that he was not who he said he was. Till date, I think he is married or maybe has kids of his own, though he has denied it till today.

A SHORT ACQUAINTANCE

I had decided I was going to have my baby in the US. Throughout the pregnancy, he was there taking me to my hospital appointments and all, but most times I had to pay for my meds and all that because he had contracts for which payments had not cleared. The beautiful thing about my pregnancy was it was without any event. I never had morning sickness, neither was there nausea or allergy to food. I worked till the day before I left for America for the birth of my child.

I was almost 8 months gone when I travelled to the US, so all I did when my mum and I arrived in Minneapolis was shop for the baby and wait for him to come. I had decided before I left that I would have to return the engagement ring I was given because there were too many questions hanging and the more I got to discover, the more I did not know this man. The baby was two weeks over due. My due date was the 16th of August 2016, but I had to be induced on the 30th of August. I had my son on the 31st August 2016 at 3.49am. He weighed 4 kg and was such a hairy baby. It was an experience I can't explain, but even then, I could feel God holding me through it all. Because I lost some blood after the delivery, I was transfused, and we were discharged on the 1st of September.

It was exciting being a mother, and I was very grateful for my mum and her sister, my aunt. They helped ease me into motherhood, feeding him, and the late-night feeding and all. Then came the day I would never forget but am eternally grateful for. My younger sister had called us on the 9th of October midnight, or early hours Nigerian time, saying she had just had a dream of me and my son at the hospital and it did not look good. She asked that my mum please anoint me, and my son and we should pray. We did, and since Nigeria was 7 hours ahead we finally had a start. Tenth morning, we gave my son a bath as usual and went about our day. But for almost a week now, my baby had not been sleeping too well at night and when we went for the routine check-up, the doctor said it was usual and there were no issues.

At this time, we were actually getting ready to travel back to Nigeria at the end of October. So that morning I was exhausted. My mum and her sister asked me to try to have some rest during the day, so I was in the room and he had slept off with my aunt and mum. Around 2.30pm he started crying. My mum told me not to bother; that she would feed him since I had started expressing milk in a bottle as I was planning to return to work. He kept crying and, so I thought I might as well go and breastfeed him, so he could at least stop crying. As I was entering the room where he was with my mum, I heard her calling out that we should come for she did not know what was wrong with him. I entered, and my son looked at me and rolled his eyes.

My mum was like, maybe he was trying to burp, and she put him on her shoulders to burp. When she lifted him, she saw a trickle of blood from his nose.

This was when we all started to panic.

We called the ambulance and in 10 minutes they were there. They stayed for 5 minutes before we left.

I was confused and remembered my sister's dream. I called her and asked her to please pray for me and inform my other siblings to pray too.

When we got to the hospital, I remember the paramedic was on top of my son trying to resuscitate him. All I remember when I got to the emergency room is clearly hearing the Spirit of God tell me, Uki trust Me. I was like, Lord I have no other person to trust but You. The doctors and nurses were trying to resuscitate my son, but he was declared dead 5.49pm. The doctor came to tell me they had tried everything, but my son had died. I told them that my son was asleep, and he would come back from the dead. The doctor was frustrated and left me, and they gave me my son to hold for two hours. I prayed and called him back to life, believing that God could bring him back. My aunt's pastors and members from her church came to pray too. After a while, I was told that I had to lay him on the bed and not touch him again for he would be taken to the medical examiners – and there were detectives who were waiting to speak to my mum, myself and my aunt since he had not been sick beforehand.

When we got home, the detectives were already at the premises; they called me in first and asked me to walk them through what had happened earlier. I told them, and then it was my mum's turn. After that they said they were so sorry for my loss and gave the number of the medical examiners. I can't say how I coped with the heart break other than to say that God upheld me with the power of his mighty hand. When my son's father was told of the demise I had finally made up my mind that we did not have anything in common. He did not make any financial contribution toward my trip and all, and I decided to start over again. I buried my son on the 28th of October 2016, 4 days before our planned departure from America.

Grateful for life, I know I will see my son again in heaven and what a catching up it will be! He had begun to smile and follow me around with his eyes. He had also begun to recognize my voice when I come into a place and maybe, when he was crying, he stopped when he heard my voice. I am so sure he had a great welcome party with my grandmother and my brothers and sisters I never got to meet (a story for another book).

I stayed in the US for three extra months to clear my head and make sense of the death of my son. The autopsy did not come up with much. All I can say is God held me and kept me sane or I would have lost my mind.

CONCLUSION

I got back to Nigeria and my son's father thought I had been lying about the death of my son. He said there was no way my son died. He said that he got it from reliable source that his son was still alive.

I wondered how I could ever have gotten involved with someone who would not even believe in my integrity because his was questionable.

I have come to the realization that I had the love I have always needed most in my life: the love of the Almighty God who sticks closer than a brother; One who knows the intention of every heart. I am not searching for Mr Right anymore. I know that if I lean into God and trust Him in all my ways, He would in truth direct my path. Marriage is a good thing; the Bible calls it an honorable thing and we must keep the bed undefiled. It's a shame that today men and women are no longer people of integrity. They say what they don't mean and are self-centered and so selfish in life. We have to be careful how we choose friends and how we relate with people.

My heart song and love story has just begun, for the one who keeps me neither slumbers nor sleeps.

ABOUT THE AUTHOR

Uki Asemota is a loving and soft-spoken lady who loves God and insists that her relationship with Him, through Jesus Christ, shaped her into who she is today. She longs to lead a life that fulfills the mandate Jesus gave that He came that we might have life and have it more abundantly. She loves love and believes that love is a decision and we should all decide to walk in love daily.

CONTACT

Website: www.ukiasemota.com
Email. ukiasemota@gmail.com

LOVE UNBOXED: AN ANTHOLOGY BY WOMEN FOR WOMEN

PART FOUR

ABUSE, PAIN, FEAR AND FREEDOM

THE JOURNEY IS THE DESTINATION
Lucy Arenberg: United States

"We must be willing to let go of the life we have planned so as to have the life waiting for us."

~ E.M. Forster

ARE I AM?

"Mommy, are I am?" I remember asking my mother this silly question…Relentlessly asking her. Driving her crazy because she had no idea what I meant. The grammatically incorrect question amused her, however to my 4-year-old self it was perfectly legitimate to ask my mom to tell me who I was. Finally, after weeks of asking her, "are I am?" she laughed and provided an answer, "Lucy, you're not making much sense." She'd often tell my dad that I inherited her sense of humor, but in reality, no one compared to my mom, she was a one-act show. For my 5th birthday she decided to throw a costume party. The entire neighborhood, family and friends were invited, and she made sure everyone roared with laughter. My mother was funny, kind, caring and always made me feel special. I adored her. Basically, she could do no wrong and I clung to her like a baby koala bear.

And so, my childhood progressed, however, my mom's answer to my earlier question began to manifest as my life started to "not make much sense." The years that followed were filled with turmoil; divorcing parents, emotional and mental anguish, sexual abuse, drug abuse, an eating disorder, and probably most damaging -- a severed relationship with my mother. The days of asking myself the elusive question, "are I am?" slowly came to an end. I grew from a bright, confident, happy child into a panic ridden, drug addicted, and completely lost version of myself by the time I was 21years old.

Around the age of 6, I became painfully aware of ongoing battles between my parents. One in particular involved smashing dishes and screaming voices. While my older brother and I silently ate breakfast, I glanced at him - our eyes glued to one another, as if trying to comfort each other, I knew then he felt as confused and as scared as I did. My brother would come to be a source of connection and strength to me, to the insanity that was beginning to unfold in our family. However later, he initially denied, at least outwardly, our father's indiscretions toward me.

After months of screaming parents, flying dishes, tears, and angry outbursts, I began to shut down emotionally and mentally. My mother was agonizing in her own pain, and was no longer the mom who laughed with me or comforted me when I needed her. The visceral pain I experienced was enough to force me to retreat to my bedroom as much as I could. I became a recluse, basically only coming out to eat or use the bathroom. Then rather abruptly, we packed up our belongings, loaded furniture onto a truck and moved from our tiny home to an even smaller apartment in the suburbs. But one thing was missing…my mom.

My father had my mother committed involuntarily to Chicago Read Mental Hospital – a state funded psychiatric institution. Her diagnosis was manic depression with schizoaffective disorder. It's funny I never really thought of my mom as crazy or mentally ill when I was young. To me, she was just my charismatic mother with a fantastic imagination that loved me as much as I loved her. But the divorce court judge ruled in my dad's favor and he was awarded sole custody of my brother and I. Sadly, what the judge didn't know was that my father was a functional alcoholic whose disease would only intensify during the next 20 years.

After the divorce was finalized I saw my mother weekly; every Sunday from 9am – 7pm at her studio apartment. Despite being fully medicated for her mental illness, her appearance and demeanor terrified me. She was no longer the vibrant, fun-loving, beautiful woman I knew as my mom. Instead she spoke to invisible people, rarely showered, and would look at me with a blank, soulless expression, as if another entity inhabited her body. During one of my Sunday visits, I remember vividly a taxi picking us up and driving us to one of the most expensive hotels in Chicago. My mom, brother and I sat in the lobby for what felt like hours until finally my mother started swearing and cursing my dad's name at the top of her lungs. I watched her in horror until I couldn't stand it anymore and I ran out of the lobby into the street looking for someone, anyone, to take me away. Eventually the concierge kicked us out. I cried myself to sleep that night determined to stuff the memory into the furthest corners of my mind.

I used to tell people that I lost my mom when I was 7 years old. The trust, security, love and basic "mothering" I used to feel from her was replaced with her calling me names, belittling me, insulting me, and speaking nonsense. Yet at the same time, I saw sparks of normalcy on occasion I knew my mother was still there, somewhere in her body. But the medication and her mental state imprisoned her to a life of disconnect...from herself, from others, from reality. At times, she tried to reconnect with me as best she could, but it was too late. My emotional attachment to her felt permanently severed.

Later in life and after years of therapy I discovered that detaching from her when I was a child was a form of self-protection. As an adult, I never really allowed anyone to get close to me. I subconsciously learned that people were untrustworthy. A firmly rooted belief that I had to protect myself was established deep within my psyche. It wasn't until many years later that I learned my mother's medication was never regulated properly and that resulted in her erratic behavior. But by then, the emotional damage had been done. In my mind, I no longer had a mom, but just a woman I was obligated to visit once per week, on Sundays, from 9am to 7pm for the next 10 years of my life.

BEYOND RECKLESS

Back at home, life with my father went from bad to worse. His alcohol consumption increased dramatically. He was very much a binge drinker and would get drunk daily for weeks and then abstain, only to relapse again a month later. In hindsight, I discovered that my own binge eating disorder stems directly from my dad's binge drinking. I used food to self-soothe liked he used alcohol to deal with depression and masking his emotional anguish. As my father became more emotionally withdrawn and verbally abusive toward me, I felt like I was walking on eggshells in that apartment and I grew to fear him. Anything could set my father off on a hostile, verbal rampage; not cleaning the dishes fast enough, not keeping the house clean enough, or not finishing my dinner. Instead of communicating like a normal person he'd yell and drink himself into a stupor and stumble into bed.

And then it happened. The incestual abuse from my father that colored my life on and off for the next 3 years. Around the age of 13, my dad started to notice the "womanly" changes happening to my body. He'd make lewd, objectifying comments about my body, "You're so vivacious, Lucy, you're beautiful, stunning," he used to say, and stare at me with lust in his eyes. I felt disgusted. One night after a drinking binge, he crossed the line and grabbed me by my waist and pulled me onto his lap. I've subconsciously blocked out the exact details of his assault on me, but I do remember him trying to kiss me while sitting on his lap and me struggling to get away.

The next morning, he'd shamefully ask for my forgiveness for, "his inappropriate behavior," he would say. And me, always replying, "It's ok, dad." Only to have this scenario repeated for several more years. I felt trapped, angry, disgusted and revengeful. But mostly I was ashamed. I told no-one of what my father was doing. I cannot say with certainty his sexual advances happened weekly or even monthly as I've stuffed his violations toward me deep into my

subconscious. Regardless of the exact number of times, I was violated emotionally, mentally, and physically and my father became another person I couldn't trust.

Sometime during my mid-teens, I tried to have a conversation with my brother about what happened to me during our father's binge drinking episodes. He'd come home occasionally for visits from college and I'd broach the subject carefully, "Dad abused me," I'd say, and his response was dismissive, as if he couldn't fathom our father doing this. With my brother choosing to ignore what transpired, I plunged into depression. I wanted to break free from my father, from my life, but I had nowhere to go...except down... into a world of drugs and promiscuity which temporarily numbed my pain.

My teenage years were marred with cocaine and marijuana use. I'd leave home to "party" for days on end. To say I was "boy crazy" was an understatement. I turned to drugs and sex to ease my troubled life. My drunk father and insane mother could not see what their daughter had become. Eventually, my father kicked me out of the house when I was 17. I was angry, but also relieved to be gone from his uncomfortable stares and objectifying comments. His sexual advances toward me stopped at this time. Probably because I showed so much disdain toward him and was never home. I ended up moving into my mother's apartment. I also attended cosmetology school which was in conjunction with my high school studies. I received my license to work as a hairstylist at the same time I (barely) graduated high school.

Living with my mom was actually a reversal of roles, as I became a mother to her. I'd grocery shop, cook and ensure that she swallowed her required daily medication. However, despite my best intentions, the hallucination & delusions she experienced were getting worse. She would often set the table with a place setting for Jesus. Many times she'd forget to turn off the gas stove and the apartment filled with noxious fumes. She also lived in a bathrobe for weeks. I learned to read the signs that my mom's medication needed to be adjusted, and that required me to lure her into my car so I could get her checked into the nearest mental hospital.

During this time cocaine use was still a regular part of my life. I needed it to cope, to escape, to feel... anything. Yet, I now know that an unseen, loving force was guiding me and protecting me. Little did I know I was only a few years away from recognizing and surrendering to a higher power, learning to forgive, and most importantly understanding my own power to help radically alter my destiny.

INTO THE LIGHT

Just before my 21st birthday, I applied for a job with Carnival Cruise Lines to work as a hairstylist on board ship. Two months later, I landed the position and was off to Miami. By accepting the job, a cascade of events was set in motion that changed the trajectory of my life. Never in my wildest dreams did I imagine that I could escape my life and begin fresh somewhere else. But there I was, on the SS Holiday ready to embark on a high seas adventure. I was happy. Free. It felt as if the salty ocean air was cleansing me from my dirty past. I loved every single moment on that ship. My days were filled with cutting and styling passenger's hair, and at night I meandered the huge ship with my cabin mates and enjoyed dancing & socializing. Life was good. And then one evening, the dreaded white powder appeared. A crew member asked if I liked to party... I felt powerless to resist. Except this time, I snorted too much of it. The mound of cocaine was almost as big as the one in the last scene of Al Pacino's "Scar

Face." I came close to losing my life that night. But what happened the following morning was most definitely a rebirth.

A friend of mine witnessed my drug binge and stayed with me the entire night. I refused to get help from the ship's doctor and instead prayed with her. On my knees, begging God to forgive me, I promised that if I made it through the night alive I would never touch drugs again. God responded and I'm still here. As hard as it was to give up, I've never looked back. I chose to create a new life for myself. I learned to embrace my past, process repressed fearful emotions, and release them to a higher power. I learned to meditate which ultimately saved me. I discovered the words, "I am" in many religious traditions is another name for God. In all ways possible, I had come full circle to my initial question when I was a child, "are I am?" And now I had my answer – I was indeed connected to a higher power and felt love, peace and joy for the first time in many years. Meditation, the purposeful act of going within has nourished my soul, and led me to self-forgiveness and self-love. It set me on a path to freedom.

I proudly proclaimed, "The cycle of dysfunction ends with me." And it did. I became a voracious learner of spirituality, the mind-body connection, and the healing and restorative power of surrendering my pain to God and following and trusting my personal intuition. I lost my mother to suicide on July 19, 2001.

Yet, I know she's with me, as I feel her loving presence guiding me on my life's journey. My father stopped drinking in 1992. He attends alcoholics anonymous meetings and has been sober ever since. We have a cordial relationship and communicate occasionally. My brother has now accepted what happened to me with care and compassion. Forgiveness is key. It's a life-long daily process, but living in gratitude, and truly knowing and embracing my own power, I've learned to co-create my life to one of peace, joy, beauty and optimism.

ABOUT THE AUTHOR

Lucy Arenberg is the founder and Director of LifeSpark Healing Arts Center and is a certified mind-body coach and master holistic energy practitioner. She gently assists clients to compassionately process and release emotionally charged events that contributes to physical pain or disease, depression and anxiety. The power of forgiveness, reframing, energy body work and implementing positive psychology are the core components of her practice. She's currently completing her Masters of Science Degree in Clinical Psychology from Benedictine University. She lives in the Chicago area with her husband and two children.

CONTACT

Website: www.lifesparkcenter.com
Email: lucyaren@mac.com

THE PARENT'S LOTTERY
Blake Taylor: United States

"The connections between and among women are the most feared, the most problematic, and the most potentially transforming force on the planet"

~ Adrienne Rich

HOW IT BEGAN

It is so true that we learn what we live. If you were lucky in the parent's lottery, you won the jackpot. You were born to two healthy people in a healthy relationship. You very likely have had a happy childhood and a happy life. In this scenario, you will have developed a great self-esteem and self-worth. I wasn't so lucky and didn't win the parent's lottery.

I was born to a narcissist father. He was the president of a Chicago bank. He was very successful in his career. He was all about making money and his famous friends. He had many of what they now call "sugar babies." He was not interested in his wife, nor his children.

I was very young when my parents divorced. I have one sister, four years younger than me. My mother was a stay at home mom. I think my mother was a good mother before the divorce, but I'm not even sure. After the divorce, my mother began a nursing job.

My father was not in my life in any meaningful way before and after the divorce. He was emotionally vacant. He was incapable of empathy. He reminded me of a robot. After the divorce, he paid the child support, and that's about it. When I did see him, it was on a Sunday afternoon to visit his mother or to drop my sister and me off at the roller rink. He never said much.

My mother hated my father. She would often tell me that I reminded her of him. I felt how much she disliked me; it was palpable. My sister looked a lot like my mother and acted like her. They were close. To this day they are close. To this day I still hear that I remind my mother of my father. I limit my exposure to this very unhealthy woman.

My childhood was misery. I was mentally and physically abused by my mother. My father knew and did nothing to extricate me from this situation. I was also sexually molested by my best friend's father. In those days it wasn't talked about like it is now. I didn't understand what was happening to me. I finally found the courage to tell my mother.

I will never forget her response. The man that was molesting me was the president of the condo board where we lived. My mother exclaimed, "You didn't tell anyone, did you? I don't want to be kicked out of our condo." I felt so frightened and confused. I used to cry myself to sleep at night. My mother would still send me to play at my friend's condo knowing that her father was molesting me. I used to dream of the day when I would turn 18 and escape my life. I know for certain that any adult never loved me as a child. As a result of my abusive childhood, I had no self-esteem and no self-worth which set me up for a great deal of pain during many years that followed. In being a child who is being mentally, physically and sexually abused, I believed that I had no value as a human being.

A NEW LIF E

When I was growing up I would dream of the life that I was going to have when I was old enough to leave home. I would dream of how my Prince Charming would find me. He would truly love me and protect me. We would have children and grow old together. I grew up in such a dysfunctional environment that I honestly wouldn't even know what that looked like. However, I needed to hold on to that belief to get through the childhood that I was living.

One day I met a man, Mark, who said all the right things to me. He would later ask me to marry him. He made all the promises to me that I had always dreamed of hearing. He promised to be a loving husband and that he would cherish me forever. He promised me that we would have the happy life that I had always dreamed of. He sounded like that Prince Charming that I believed one day would find me. He was not at all physically the type of man that I would normally be attracted to, but he made up for that in what I saw as exactly the kind of man that I would find true happiness. That was all that mattered. His looks were not important to me. I was so happy and believed that this is the man that I was going to be blissfully happy with for the rest of my life. I believed that the life I was about to embark upon was going to make me forget my abusive and painful childhood.

I had been a crime victim and was in crime victim counseling at the beginning of my relationship with Mark. I was able to discuss my childhood with this therapist. This was the beginning of a long journey of self-discovery and healing. Having been a crime victim ended up being a blessing in disguise in that it brought me to this therapist.

I was a court reporter, and Mark was in medical school when we met. Mark finished his training and became a surgeon. We were married in a private ceremony in a cute little church. We only went on a weekend honeymoon because we were busy with his medical practice. I was so very happy and excited about our future together.

Over the years and through the therapy with my crime victim therapist I learned that I had married a narcissist, just like my father. The similarities were shocking. How did I not see this? I was married to a man that was all about himself; a man that was all about money; a man that there was no emotional connection to, a man that was incapable of empathy. Just like my father, I married a person who felt like a robot. I was lonely and unhappy.

I worked for many years in Mark's clinics. I felt like we made good business partners, but the marriage was so empty. Mark had achieved success in his career and was making two million dollars a year when we separated. I asked him to go to divorce counseling with me in hopes that we could keep anger out of the divorce. I had hoped that we could have an amicable divorce and treat each other kindly and fairly. We had spent two decades together, this wasn't much to ask for in ending our marriage. Mark refused. I asked him several more times to go to this type of counseling because I had spoken to some people that this worked for. He continued to refuse.

Nothing could have prepared me for the acrimonious divorce that would follow. I never would have imagined that Mark could be capable of the kind of cruelty that he has inflicted upon me throughout this divorce. Mark told me in an email early in our separation that he would drag the divorce out for years and bankrupt me in attorney's fees. He hired an attorney who is an 80-year-old misogynist, known for representing rich men and abusing the estranged wife throughout the process.

I had been stalked for over a year by a guy who had his private investigator's license revoked during this entire time, hired by Mark. The stalker took pictures and videos of me. This stalker terrified me and is currently under investigation for stalking me.

After spending two years in divorce court and being called nasty names, lied about and disrespected every time we were before the judge I decided to go public with my story. As a child, I couldn't do anything to stand up for myself through all the abuse that I endured. I got to a point in this divorce that I said enough is enough. I will no longer sit back in silence and be abused. I decided to set boundaries that I will no longer let Mark and his attorneys cross. I was ready to take my power back. I went on social media and started telling my story. I began to share what I was experiencing in divorce court. I stopped feeling like a victim and began feeling very empowered. So many women began contacting me who were going through the same abuse. A real sisterhood formed, and we started calling ourselves the Soul Sisters.

Narcissists do not like their bad behavior to be known, and Mark was no exception. He filed a defamation lawsuit against me for going public with my divorce. I have now spent two years defending my right to free speech. Mark has his divorce attorney and another law firm representing him in this lawsuit. Just like in divorce court I have been lied about to this judge. My attorney's fees have been run up with their filing of nonsense motions. They have tried to silence me by making it hard to afford to defend my 1st Amendment right. The divorce attorney has routinely lied to the judge presiding over the divorce about what I have written on social media about the divorce.

Mark lost his job and stopped paying me support in

April. Mark's attorney is now claiming in divorce court that he lost his job as a result of my sharing my abusive divorce on social media.

We filed a motion for summary judgment to have the defamation case against me dismissed. The judge ruled in our favor and dismissed the case. I have not defamed anyone and am simply sharing what I am going through in this divorce. The whole thing is available online through the clerk's office website. I'm still perplexed at being sued for this. Sadly, you can be sued for just about anything by someone who wants to control you.

It has now been four years since the filing of the divorce. I have been forced to spend over $500,000.00 on attorney's fees. There is no end in sight. Mark has done exactly as he promised in his email to me four years ago. He has drug this divorce out for years and is causing me to have a hard time affording my attorneys. I'm not bankrupt yet.

THE NEW AND IMPROVED ME

Sometimes from your biggest adversities comes your biggest opportunities. I am stronger than I've ever been in my life. I know my self-worth and will never settle for less than I deserve. I've joined forces with many women's groups and advocates for family court reform. I will spend the rest of my life working to change our broken family law system. I enjoy helping other women get through what I have gone through and survived. I've been blessed to meet and work with very courageous women who I will remain connected to for the rest of my life.

It took going through everything that I've been through from my childhood through my marriage to Mark to become the woman that I am today. I still often talk with my crime victim therapist all these years later. She is amazing and the reason I got to this place of healing and closure.

I finally met my Prince Charming. They do exist. I learned what a healthy man looks like and what a healthy relationship feels like. I finally know what it feels like to truly be loved and to truly love someone back. You really can have a happily ever after.

ABOUT THE AUTHOR

As a result of her very brutal divorce, Blake has become passionate about causing change to the very antiquated laws in family court. She works with women's groups and many like-minded people fighting for this change.

In 2014 Blake was diagnosed with postural orthostatic tachycardia syndrome (POTS). This is an autonomic nervous system dysfunction. There is no cure. There is no FDA approved medication for this. Blake is involved in bringing awareness to this illness.

CONTACT

Website: Www.MsBlakeTaylor.com
Email: MsBlakeTaylor2@gmail.com

BEHIND THE LOOKING GLASS
Penny Hollick: United States

"Someone I loved once gave me a box full of darkness. It took me years to understand that this, too, was a gift."

~ Mary Oliver

HOW DID I END UP HERE?

I am sitting on a swinging bench enjoying the warmth from the sun rays shining down on me and enjoying the solitude. This bench is not an ordinary swinging bench. This bench is on the grounds of a large mental institution and part of the alcoholism rehabilitation unit. I am a patient here, and I'm still trying to figure out my life, and how I ended up here at my young age of 37 years old! This place is for drunks and very sick people.

I had always dreamed of doing something special with my life. I was a straight A student; I earned a B.S. degree in Accounting from California Polytechnic University in Pomona, California and graduated with honors. I was married to the most handsome Italian man. We had four beautiful children together in a short span of five years. I had owned my own accounting business, and I currently was the Senior Auditor for the largest CPA firm in town. I owned a beautiful log home right in the woods on a beautiful lake. Life could not have been any better. I had fulfilled all of my dreams. And yet here I sat swinging on this bench, alone, and missing my children.

My alcoholic mother and workaholic father raised me, which translates into I was in charge of my three younger siblings when I was eight years old. I couldn't trust my mother or father to watch over them. I saved my brother from strangulation one day when he was hanging in between his crib bars. At that very moment, my mom and dad were sitting in the kitchen arguing and ignoring the screaming of their son. That is when I knew I had to take charge of my family. I hated alcohol and swore that I would never be like my mother.

My heart was in my throat as I thought about all of the relatively recent agonizing events in my life. I knew I wouldn't cry because I would never allow myself to cry. The most I could feel was sadness and then depression. If I allowed myself to cry, the tears might never stop because of all the pain and neglect and abandonment from my childhood years. I was a strong little child and never cried then. If I came home from school and found my mother passed out on her bed from the alcohol, I would check on my siblings, do my homework, and make the best of it. When she tried to commit suicide, I didn't cry. I felt safer when the ambulance took her and my father away to the hospital. Then I knew she was in good hands, and nothing could happen to any of us. I slept very peacefully that night.

Angelo knew that my mother was an alcoholic, and, yet, he was the one who suggested that we go out bar-hopping at the weekends. Didn't he know that I would become an alcoholic? In his own words, he said, "I created a monster!" and perhaps my husband of fifteen years, was right. When I drank, I had no control over myself. I was a blackout drunk.

The first thing I thought of in the morning was What did I do last night that would cause me shame? I hated myself. I hated Angelo for putting me up to this. Anything I did, I had to excel at it – even if I was on a self-destruct path.

I seem to be on a roll here with my introspection. I think I will go inside the hospital to my tiny room. The counselors told us it was healing to journal our thoughts.

Now that I look back at everything that happened, Angelo was grooming me for one of his fantasies. He may have temporarily received the outcome that he desired, but ultimately his plan backfired on him. He never counted on me losing my inhibitions when I drank and receiving the courage to stand up to him and tell him "No!" for once.

THE MOST INTRIGUING ITALIAN MAN OF MY DREAMS

You wouldn't understand any of this because you don't know how I was when Angelo and I first met seventeen years ago. I was barely 21 years old, and he was 26. I was going to college and working part time; he soon got a job and began working full time. At the weekends, we would hang out and party with his three cousins and their girlfriends.

Angelo overwhelmed me with his attention and affection. Sometimes he would say things to make fun of me, jokingly, in front of his cousins. I would laugh along with everyone else, but it did hurt me inside. A person would never know, though, because I had learned at a very young age to be "The Great Pretender." I learned never to show my emotions and never to cry.

I saw Angelo's Italian temper flare when we were driving in the beach cities. If another driver cut him off in traffic, Angelo would blare his horn and had his finger flying high out the window. He would stick his head out the window and yell out the foulest obscenities one could imagine. I would just sit there quietly. He invented "road rage" in the 1970's, and I felt the same nervous stomach return that I always had as a child.

One day Angelo shared a secret with me. He told me that he was depressed and often thought of suicide. This big, strong macho Italian man had thoughts like that? Then another time when we were snuggling in bed together just enjoying our intimacy and togetherness, he would begin talking to me in this tiny, little voice that sounded like a small boy's voice perhaps age five years old.

When I first heard this voice, I thought that he was just silly. However, he used it on many occasions. This was a secret voice inside of him that he would never show to anyone else but me; therefore, I felt that I was a very special person to him. I felt such sadness for him when he told me these things. Well, that just hooked me right in and made me feel all the closer to him. With all of the experience that I had with my dysfunctional family, I felt certain that I could help him. I would treat him as if he were a "king," and I would make him feel so happy!

We lived together for about six months before we got married. Angelo was working full time in the stressful sales department for a large corporation. I was still going to college and working part time. I noticed a change in him in that he had brought his "road rage" into our home, and now all of those filthy, lewd remarks were being directed at me.

One night I came home after a long, hard day. Angelo was standing there waiting for me waving this envelope in the air.

And I knew just what it was.

He started screaming at me, "HOW HARD IS IT TO REMEMBER TO WALK OVER TO THAT F**KING FRONT OFFICE AND PAY OUR G-D RENT ON TIME?! I LEFT THE CHECK RIGHT THERE ON THE COUNTER FOR YOU! IF YOU HAD ANY BRAINS, YOU'D BE DANGEROUS!!"

When I cleaned the kitchen after a meal, I had to put the dishcloth in a certain place on the counter, and I had to make sure that I loaded the dishwasher a certain way. The plates facing inward on the bottom, all the glasses on the top, and all the silverware had to be standing straight up.

If I forgot and loaded a couple of plates wrong, he would yell at me "HOW MANY TIMES DO I HAVE TO TELL YOU TO LOAD THEM, SO THEY ARE ALL FACING INWARD?! WHAT ARE YOU, STUPID? WHAT A F**KING MORON YOU ARE!" He would say all of this screaming at me, and he was usually right in my face. I would look down because I could not stand to see the evil contortion in his face or the hatred spewing from his eyes.

His outbursts made me feel very sad. I must not be doing a good enough job of making him happy. I would have to try harder.

I would quietly respond, "Okay, okay, I am sorry. I won't do it again." I would say anything just to get him to calm down. I believe that I was willing to put up with these temper tantrums due to the fact that he admitted to me about his depression and suicidal thoughts. I was so much in love with all of the good parts to this man that I was willing to overlook the screaming scenes now and again to keep the peace. I noticed that I started to feel quite anxious and fearful. I was clueless as to the existence of the concept that I had a right to set up my "personal boundaries." Looming large was a sinister black cloud over my head as to what my future destiny would hold by my lack of this knowledge.

With all that I had learned in college, I had never learned anything about verbal or psychological abuse. I did know that when a man beat up his wife, this was physical abuse. I had no red warning flags that went up in my mind. My brother told me one day that Angelo treated me with no respect. All I could respond was "you just don't understand everything."

THE WORLD REVOLVES AROUND ANGELO

As the years went by, the verbal and psychological abuse escalated. We moved out of warm southern California to a small town in a northern State that was near the Canadian border. We made this major move because it was Angelo's dream to be a professional sled dog racer. We ended up with eighty (yes, 80!) Alaskan Huskies in the dog lot so that he could train his sled dog teams. In the Winter, he would go on the sled dog racing circuit.

He drove his truck with his dogs all the way across Canada, the Yukon, and ended up in Fairbanks, AK. He would stop and race his teams all along the way. Of course, I was left at home alone with our four young children: new-born, 16 months old, three years old and four years old. He left the sixty Huskies who did not make his team with me! We lived in a State where the high temperature for the day was thirty degrees below zero! I was so mentally sick that I saw nothing wrong with this, and I allowed him to leave me home alone with all of this responsibility.

I lost more than my self-esteem living with this man. I lost my identity. He was an emotional vampire who sucked up my soul. He was so controlling that he even wanted to know what was in my mind. He would ask me every day "What are you thinking about?"

By now, I hated him. He had driven away all of the love that I had once felt so deeply for him. I felt like I was walking on eggshells all the time in our house because I was on edge waiting for the next big blow up. There was only one time I could predict his rage, and that was when he drove down our driveway to get the mail. If he was expecting a check in the mail from a customer, and it was not in the mailbox, all hellfire and brimstone would break loose in our home. He would rant and rave, yell, scream and swear using worse words than he used before. All of this right in front of his four young children. I did tell him not to do this in front of our kids. He never listened.

NEVER GIVE UP – YOU CAN OVERCOME

Many more abusive incidents happened during my marriage to a Narcissistic Personality Disorder (NPD), or Psychopath, or Sociopath. Every therapist that I have worked with has used one of the above names to describe Angelo. The people like Angelo never receive a diagnosis because they never seek treatment; there is nothing wrong with them in their mind. There is a myriad of dynamics going on in any abusive relationship. To use the most concise, descriptive words, I will quote Bree Bonchay, LLSW:

Relationship with a Narcissist in a Nutshell:
>You will go from being the perfect love of their life
>To nothing you do is ever good enough
>You will give your everything
>And they will take it all
>And give you less and less in return
>You will end up depleted
>Emotionally, Mentally, Spiritually,
>And probably Financially,
>And then get blamed for it all.

CONCLUSION

Women or men (this goes both ways), if I have said anything in my story that made you feel uncomfortable inside or gave you a little shiver, please listen to my words. The abuse will only get worse. It will never get better. If you suspect that you may be in an abusive domestic relationship, the sooner that you can escape, the better off you will be. There are local and national organizations now you can call for help.

ABOUT THE AUTHOR

I am a Survivor of child abuse/neglect, growing up with an alcoholic mother, marriage to an NPD, alcoholism and recovery, depression, and anxiety. Rather than dealing with my issues, I stuffed each trauma inside my body in its separate box. In this way, I could still function as a mother, a self-employed accountant, and a friend.

However, I still had to face one more giant obstacle as recent as the year 2013. This was, without a doubt, the biggest hurdle I would force myself to push through.

I have made this my mission: to help educate and empower all women who have experienced any or all of the traumas that I have overcome. Therapy introduced me to the person I was created to be from the beginning. Do not listen to your doctor who tells you that you will never recover. We all have the power inside of us to be an OVERCOMER and a THRIVER. You become what you think, and you also become what you speak. There is no room in our brains for any negative thinking. Make a practice of listening to your self-talk.

I have intentionally left out the powerful ending to my story. You can read my entire story in my "educational" memoir, My Naked Face, set up to be published November 2017. I will also write about this in the next anthology to be released in the spring of 2018, entitled Believe.

CONTACT

Website: http://pennyhollick.com/
https://twitter.com/PennyHollick

DARKEST HOURS
Jay Jay Williams: United Kingdom

"It's easy to be independent when you've got money, but to be independent when you haven't got a thing - that's the Lord's test".

~ Mahalia Jackson

When you look at me
today what do you see?
The weak vulnerable
person you made me out
to be!
Today I stand proud for
what I've achieved, I grew
strong, found courage and
faith, a sense of belief.

After 17 long intimidating
years your abuse took its
toll,
you tried to kill me,
drug me and took all my
control.
I was living in a prison,
dying a slow death, but
to the outside world I
appeared lucky, with no
distress.
The domestic violence
was affecting our three
beautiful sons,
their health and happiness
were suffering: they were
under your thumb.

I couldn't paper over it
or minimise it any longer
with toys
I didn't want them to be a
product of you or turn out
to be dangerous boys.

I hated you for what you
had made me become my
motherly instincts had to
succumb.
Why couldn't you love me
the way it was supposed
to be?
And we could all live
together as a happy family.
If you want to be a single
parent, I'll take everything
from you; no one will want
you
when I've finished with
you.
Goodbye

SUNDAY EVENING

It was a bright, sunny day outside our lovely big home but inside the storm was brewing. Today was going to be a life changing day for all of us: Paul was leaving the family home. It wasn't meant to be this way. Our family would be broken forever; no going back. I had called Paul's father up to our home in Norbury to help with the situation, because I was petrified of Paul and knew he wouldn't hit me in front of his father. But his degrading humiliation showed no bounds. Pointing in my face, ridiculing and laughing at me, I wondered why I ever loved this evil man. I felt like a failure, depressed, weak, embarrassed and broken. But I knew this dark cloud would pass, for the stars always shine in the darkness.

The front door closed, and Paul left with his father and some belongings. We were finally free. It had been such an emotional day filled with such heartbreak and pain. After having been managed by intimidation my whole life, the relief was overwhelming. No longer did my children have to live in fear and darkness, seeing and hearing things no child should have to live with. I was their mother and I was going to protect them with my life, nurture them and shower them with my unconditional love. I became emotionally withdrawn and the only way I now felt pain was when my children were hurting.

Paul couldn't hurt me anymore and the children didn't have to see the violence and the trauma. We were all finally safe and we could start a new, happy, fearless life. I could shower them with peace and happiness.

I put on the music, danced and called the boys down. Luke, now 16, Joseph 8 and Elijah 5 ½. I explained that Paul had left, that he loved them dearly and that he had only moved ten minutes away. He would still be a big part of their lives and he would see them every other week. We didn't need to live in fear anymore. I had tried so hard to make the relationship work, but I was powerless. Powerless over Paul's actions yet responsible for putting my children through such trauma. I wanted to spare my children the stigma of being in a single parent family and not having the love of a father. I had always wanted a father in my life and now my children were losing theirs. I had put 17 years of blood sweat and tears into this relationship. It was all I knew. But I also knew it wasn't right. I tried every possible way to make it work but choice was taken out of my hands by the shock of the Speech Therapist's diagnosis saying that our three sons' speech impediment was caused by the living conditions of domestic violence at home. I hadn't even told the therapist my situation!

BUILDING RESILIENCE

The freedom of laughter from my boys brought joy

and happiness to me, and I basked in the delight of not having to be submissive to Paul anymore. It was lovely being able to have the boys' friends around for dinner after school and have sleepovers, trips to theme parks and holidays Finally I could come out of isolation, come out of my prison in which I'd been living, and start rebuilding my life.

Our peace and harmony was short lived, gone was the physical abuse but the emotional abuse was growing by the day. Myself and the boys were punished by exclusion from Paul's family, and Paul would not turn up on time for the boys – or not even turn up at all. When he did, he would either take Joseph and Elijah and not Luke, or Luke and Joseph and not Elijah. It was incredibly insensitive and so hurtful leaving one of the boys. He was the father of his three sons, yet he was too busy womanising and looking after himself to be interested in his responsibilities. This caused even greater distress. My children would be ready, bags packed, waiting for daddy, looking out of the window. But daddy wouldn't come. He would phone and say something had come up and he'd be there tomorrow. Tomorrow would never come.

I would pretend to the boys that his car had broken down, only for Joseph to say, 'Why doesn't he get the AA to fix it like he did when we were with him?' It was heart-breaking watching my children cry for their father, and I carried enormous guilt from this.

Paul wouldn't listen to me no matter how hard I tried explaining. He wanted to ruin me and this was the only way he could hurt me: making me pay through him hurting my children. He had so many negative influences in his life. He knew that when he had the children I could go out and do what I wanted and this he didn't want. He was still trying to control me from a distance, telling me I was his and he would never love anyone else the way he loved me. He kept trying it on, pinching my bum whenever he could, until I decided enough was enough.

I was at home one day and I received a visit from a Social Worker, she was checking my situation out as the Speech Therapist had referred me! I explained that Paul had left and that my boys weren't at risk from domestic violence anymore, I showed her around the house and she left satisfied.

The boys' general health started improving in our more relaxed living environment. However, the inherent stress or lack of Paul's fatherly skills was hard to adjust to and understand. I was tormented inside. Soon after Paul left I started receiving phone calls from our mutual friends telling me a heroin addict was pregnant by him. I was mortified. Why the hell wasn't he practising safe sex! I felt completely betrayed. I didn't want my boys to know because it would shatter their world, so I told Paul not to tell them about the pregnancy yet; that it was better coming from me. On the morning of Luke's GCSEs, Paul decided to ring him at 8.00am and tell him about the pregnancy. I felt like I was having a breakdown! Depressed, I couldn't take anymore. I was powerless, yet I had to find the strength within to be strong for my boys. My health got worse. I developed fibromyalgia alongside my spinal problems from the severe kicks I had received (Paul used to kick me in the back because it was the only place people couldn't see). I developed a brain tumour and felt physically broken.

I surprised my son Luke with a limousine for his 16th birthday to take him and his friends to London. He had been through so much and took on the responsibility of helping with his younger brothers so well. My friend Michelle, who had become their adopted auntie, paid half of the money for the car. She wanted to cheer him up as we had been abandoned by the rest of the family. I felt so proud of Luke when he was getting into the car. He looked beautiful and dressed to perfection. Yet I felt so sad that Paul wasn't there to see his son off. The pain was so raw inside me and I felt so hurt. Why was this happening to me?

Paul's baby was born and the mother, being addicted to heroin, ran off and left the baby with him. He rang me and begged for us to get back together and be a family again. He reminded me of how much I had really wanted a daughter and that the baby's mother was not interested. So, this would be a perfect opportunity for us to get back together. I told him I would think about it and let him know in a few days. I had no intentions whatsoever of getting back together with him, but I wanted him to believe there was a chance just to hurt him like I was hurting. He kept calling me and begging me, and eventually I told him I would never get back with him as he had called the child Whitney. It was the same name I had called our son Elijah while I had been pregnant when I thought I was having a girl. I asked Paul why he chose the name Whitney and he said it was to hurt me! I felt sickened, deeply betrayed, So I told him I hated him, would never get back with him and for the rest of his life, whenever he calls Whitney, he can think of me as I chose the name. I put the phone down and cried a river. I had never been so hurt in my whole life. My heart felt like it had shards of glass ripping through it, shredding it to pieces. My life was so painful.

9/11/2001 ALSO MY WEEK OF HELL

I had already dropped the boys off to school when the letter arrived. Only it didn't make sense: an eviction notice from Paul's solicitor! We were to be evicted in a few weeks' time and Luke was due to start university shortly. I rushed around to my friend Maxine's house to show her the letter. She was utterly shocked! How could Paul do this to his own children? I phoned him in front of Maxine hoping he would be more amicable. He wasn't. His voice was full of contempt, pure evil. I broke down sobbing on the floor and begged him not to do it. We had nowhere else to live, no family or friends to go to and would be homeless! His next words will stay with me forever: 'You wanted to be a single parent so deal with it! They are not my children anymore and you won't be homeless because Croydon Council will put you in a hostel! Maxine hung up the phone to save me from any more shame. I went home, picked up the boys from school, took them to their activities and tried to carry on like normal. The next morning life seemed so bleak with no support from anyone. I begged Paul again not to do this and even tried offering him money. I called the council but to no avail. I was tired of fighting and felt like the biggest failure going. Where was I going to live with my children, what were we going to do? Paul owned four houses, yet he was evicting us from our family home. I lost all faith: why wasn't God helping me? I desperately needed help and support but there was none. I had hit rock bottom and couldn't see a way out. I had lost my courage and felt so weak. So, like a coward, I decided to end my life. I was desperate and couldn't take any more. I believed I would be better off dead, I felt powerless and thought it would be better for everyone if I were dead. I didn't want to die and leave my boys: it was a desperate cry for help. I didn't know what else to do, so I got a bottle of blue Smirnoff vodka and all the painkillers I had and locked myself in the bathroom. I phoned my friend Cazzie crying, and told her what I had done. She only lived around the corner from me, by the time she arrived I was unconscious, so she called the ambulance and kicked in the bathroom door I woke up the next day in Mayday hospital with Luke and Cazzie sitting beside the hospital bed. They took turns feeding me a charcoal drink, which helps the stomach in overdose situations, I felt awful. I was assigned a psychiatrist and left the hospital with the enormous guilt of what I'd just done.

The most terrible poverty is loneliness and the feeling of being unloved – Mother Teresa

A NEW DAY A NEW BEGINNING

I was lying in bed deeply depressed just two days after being discharged from Mayday hospital, when Maxine rang me, always positive she encouraged me to get up and stop moping around. so I said I would go to hers and we'd go out for a drink to try to get me out of this depressive mood. So, I drove to hers parked up, then Maxine drove us to a nearby pub in Sydenham South East London. It was a beautiful sunny evening, so we sat outside, and Maxine tried to cheer me up. Two men sitting at a table nearby joined us and bought us each a glass of wine. They seemed quite pleasant and you could tell by their physiques that they worked out in the gym a lot. I was a bit aloof and avoided any conversation at first but soon we were all chatting. When we were leaving to go home one of the guys told Maxine to follow his car as he knew a shortcut. We were unfamiliar with the route as Maxine had only just recently bought her new house there, so we decided to follow him.

I am to pay for this mistake for the rest of my life. We were driving when all of a sudden Maxine stopped behind the guy's car, he got out and was standing beside Maxine's side of the car. He asked me to get out as he wanted to give me his phone number. I stupidly got out of the car and walked towards him. He pointed to a house and said he lived there, he opened the front door and suddenly my arm was yanked. I was dragged into what turned out to be a studio flat, thrown down onto a bed while being strangled and I passed out. I regained consciousness with him on top of me, strangling me and raping me. I couldn't scream and was whispering and begging him to stop, I was going in and out of consciousness for what seemed like an eternity. I pleaded with him to stop, "no, no, please, please, please stop. My friend is outside, she's paralysed! Please stop! I have to help her!" I thought if he didn't care about me he might have shown compassion for Maxine being in a wheelchair. In the distance I could hear Maxine's horn beeping, but she was unable to get out of the car. Her wheelchair was locked in the boot!

The rest is to be continued in my new book: Resilience: my Journey from Victim to Healer.

On average two women are killed every week by domestic crime in the UK.

If you or anyone you know suffers from domestic violence and they are in an emergency, please call the police on 101 or the 24-hour National Domestic Violence Freephone Helpline (Refuge & Women's aid) on 0808 2000 247. *(JayJay's story is continuation from Love Unboxed book one)*

ABOUT THE AUTHOR

Born in 1966, England's World Cup winning year, Jay Jay Williams was one of five brothers and sisters. She experienced the hardship of an upbringing in Bermondsey, south east London, where the norm on pub doors was no blacks, no Irish & no dogs! Being of Jamaican and Irish descent, she could not understand the racial bigotry and it created an identity crisis. She had to endure 17 years of a controlling and brutally violent fiancé and when she decided to separate from him, he evicted her and their sons onto the streets of Croydon, made them homeless and abandoned them.

She is now a thriving survivor of adversity with a deep passion for helping people overcome child sexual abuse, domestic violence and trauma. Jay Jay is a freedompreneur, resilience coach, inspirational speaker, actress, mother of three sons, wife and soon to be grandmother!

CONTACT

Website: www.JayJayWilliams.com
Email: JJ-Williams@outlook.com

TRICK OR TREAT
Laura Buxo: Spain

'I could not, at any age, be content to take my place by the fireside and simply look on. Life was meant to be lived. Curiosity must be kept alive. One must never, for whatever reason, turn her back on life.'

~ Eleanor Roosevelt

DIVORCE DECISION

December 2016. Farouk had decided to travel to Egypt as he said, for thinking and being away from me just to decide what to do with his life. For me that was the end. Not because I didn't want to give him time, but just because I was really fed up with our marriage and toxic relationship. I was beginning to feel that I deserved something better in my life.

So as a step in the right direction, I wrote Love Unboxed Part One and I began to try to love and take care of myself. Believe me, it's not easy, especially when you have spent more than fifteen years without doing it. I began with little steps like going to my hairdresser more often, I bought new clothes, sometimes I wore makeup and to be sincere, I was still feeling bad about doing these things. Farouk's words were still inside me, hitting me and making me feel like I was a bitch.

So, I learned that I had to be patient with myself and give myself time just to fit in with my new life. I also went to visit a lawyer and here my insane divorce started. I was thinking that it would be something easy, you know, because we have no kids, the house is mine and the only thing that we had in common was the travel agency. Things became complicated. There were problems outside our control. After five weeks, he decided to come back home, and he thought I would accept him again. But no. I'd stopped loving him more than a year before, I was so hurt because of his psychological abuse and he was still doing it to me, every day with or without my permission.

When he arrived home, I told him I wanted the divorce, although I was really scared about his reaction. He was in shock. He started saying that he loved me so much and that he wanted another opportunity, the last one. But that was not possible. How can you ask that by shouting at me and insulting me? Even if he had asked me on bended knee, my answer would have been the same. NO. It's over.

We made a deal, we agreed to share the house until our divorce papers were ready. We began to be flatmates. What a mistake! But it seemed the only way to keep track of him, because I really feared he would walk out and disappear and I would be tied to him forever. He wasn't working, and he wasn't looking for a job either. So, you can imagine what that means. Money, money and more money from my pocket. My anxiety was getting worse again. I was feeling ill almost every day and every time I felt ill he got very angry with me, telling me that it was all about getting his attention. Again shouts, insults, words like 'you are completely crazy, nobody would want to be with you, you are weak, and a liar and I am beginning to feel fed up with you'.

FLATMATES

Even though we were just flatmates, he was still controlling my life and I wasn't happy with that. I started to say no, I said to him 'you don't own me, I have my life, I want to wear the clothes I like and makeup and perfume too. I want to go out with my friends and share some drinks and I don't need any permission. This is me, take it or leave it, wait for the papers or get out of my house, it's up to you'. He raised his hand to hit me but immediately he stopped and went for a walk.

Oh my god! I could see the anger in his face, his body language was scary, but I couldn't go back to my past. Of course, I was so scared, and I was crying like a little girl, but I had to learn to believe in me, forget about fears and believe that I could go ahead with this. I went into the bathroom and I looked in the mirror. That amazing but scared woman was me! So, I began to say to myself, 'don't give up Laura, come on, don't give up. You can do it, you are strong, don't believe in his words, believe in what you want, believe in what your heart is telling you. Don't give up'. I made the decision not to tell family and friends. I just didn't want to listen to lots of subjective opinions. I decided to put all my faith in my acupuncturist, my doctor and my psychologist and well, I couldn't talk to them every day, but I knew, and I know that they are there for me.

That night I decided to close my bedroom door using my drawer to block it. And I prayed to God that Farouk would calm down and forget what had happened before. That day I began to feel worried about my security and my life.

When I woke up the next morning and I found myself safe and sound, I just cried and felt grateful for a new day. I had to make new plans, just trying to spend as little time as possible at home, and yes, 'my' home not 'ours'. So, I started to work late at the office and he began to work as a private Arabic teacher. The funny thing was, I didn't see any money to buy food or to pay the electricity, gas, water, health insurance and phone bills. But that was normal throughout our marriage. I was the one who was always paying the bills. By this time, I didn't really want to pay anymore. I was beginning to understand that he was only using me. He was even cheating on me too. That was nothing new.

He always went to his classes with a towel, bottle of perfume and his toothbrush in his bag and when he arrived home he spent more than one hour taking a shower. What had he been doing? At this point in our marriage that was ok for me because I didn't really care, but why was he still living with me? I couldn't understand why he wasn't looking for somewhere else to live. Now I know. Who was going to pay the bills for him?

THE DIVORCE

I wanted a quick divorce and I didn't mind if I had to pay or not, I just wanted him out of my life as soon as possible. Again, he asked me for more time to find a place to go and, because the divorce papers would be delayed for more or less three months, I agreed. Once more, we made a new deal, but now with different conditions. He finally got a job and I asked him to contribute to our monthly bills. He didn't like the idea too much, but there was no other option than for him to accept.

Because I had only told my acupuncturist, my doctor and my psychologist that I was getting divorced, I explained our situation to them. My acupuncturist, a great woman who I've had several conversations with, encouraged me not to be scared, to confront the situation head on and believe in my inner power. My psychologist recommended I explain my situation to one of my brothers. He was worried that Farouk would abuse me physically, he wanted me to have someone close to me just in case. He really left me worried because he had met Farouk at the beginning of our marriage, so I knew he had a psychological profile of him.

It was a Sunday night, 28th May. I was angry because it was my father's birthday and he gave a party and invited Farouk of course. No one from my family knew what was going on yet. Farouk refused to go so rudely that he left my father feeling sad, saying besides that, it was the first day of Ramadan and he couldn't eat. I was feeling happy because he wasn't joining us but so angry by the way he talked to my father. He didn't deserve that. My parents always treated him like a son, even when, at the end, they knew everything that had happened between us.

When I arrived home after the party, Farouk wasn't there. I waited until he came back as I needed to tell him how rude he had been to my father. I wasn't able to. Why? Well he arrived home and even though he was fasting, he went to the gym for more than 2 hours. I went crazy, 'so you cannot go to a party of someone who loves you, but you go to the gym! How selfish can you get?' I left the house without saying anything while he was asking me to stay because it was time for dinner and he needed me to cook for him. I left, and I went to the park to have a walk with a friend. I came back home at midnight. He was crazy "where the f**k have you been? I was hungry, and I had to eat any old rubbish, I'm in Ramadan and you have no respect for me in this holy month. Who the hell do you think you are? Where is the woman I married?"

I just left him talking and went to my room feeling really angry and I slammed the door. Straightaway he came into my room, he grabbed me by the hair, then he took me by the shoulders and shook me violently. Finally, he pushed me and threw me onto the bed. Then he went to his room and slammed the door. I panicked, I went to the terrace just to get some air, I really was so scared. I felt that this was the last day of my life. I couldn't breathe, my heart was beating so hard, without making a sound I ran to the hospital. It was past 1am and I crossed my fingers and hoped my doctor was working that night.

When I arrived, I asked for him and the receptionist told me that he was not working, but there were more doctors. She could see how bad I was. I said, "it is ok, I will come back another day, I am fine really, thank you". I know any doctor would have helped me but at that moment I just needed him because of our mutual trust. So, because I couldn't even think straight I came back home praying for my life and I just went into my room, closed the door, blocked it again with the drawers and I asked God for a quick, painless death.

After 2 days, I realised that I had bruises on my left leg, so my lawyer recommended I go to the hospital and have it examined. I was lucky that day because my doctor was working. I was in the waiting room and he called me immediately. I still had not said a word, but I could see by his face that he knew something was seriously wrong. I could see the anger in his body language at every word I was telling him. I went to my psychologist and his reaction was the same. He advised me again to tell someone close to me. But I didn't do it. I was feeling guilty about worrying my allies. I feared that if I had told one of my brothers, he might well have flown off the handle. I decided to keep it to myself.

After a week, a good friend of ours Facetimed me and told me 'Laura, look I don't understand you. Farouk loves you very much. He has told me how much he loves you and I still cannot understand why you didn't travel with him to Egypt last December if I paid for the flight for both of you' 'What the hell are you telling me?' I answered. 'Well Laura, as you know, I have been helping you since you got married by sending money every time you needed it' 'What are you telling me? Are you pulling my leg?' I asked.

Then my friend saw that I was in shock and he sent me back all the bank transfers that he had sent to Farouk during the four years of our marriage. Not just that, but I discovered far, far worse. He had used me to get the European Community papers, Spanish nationality, he wanted to get his hands on the travel agency. He had never legalised our marriage in Egypt and that means that he's still single in his country and he had done all this without the least modicum of love for me. He didn't want to love me, he didn't need to love me... He just used me, and he did it very well.

I explained all this to my acupuncturist and she asked me, point blank, the one question I hadn't answered for myself: 'What the hell I was playing at'? That was the trigger! Everything suddenly fell into place. I wasn't scared anymore. He was an abuser, a manipulator, he was a thief, he insulted my nearest and dearest and the list goes on…Finally, finally I found the courage to order him to leave and never come back again. I was in command!

CONCLUSION

I'm so proud of my decision for divorcing him. Finally, I'm free, I've a new life. I still have some fears inside me, but I know I will be fine very soon.

I've learned that loving yourself is the clue to everything and that we can do whatever we want. We must be patient and give ourselves time to learn how to do it.

Again, treat yourself in the right way, if you don't do it, who do you think is going to?

Don't ever give up. Trust in you, trust in your possibilities. You can do it, yes, sometimes it would seem impossible but, really, if you don't give up, no one can stop you.

If you aren't feeling comfortable with some aspects of your life, you've always the chance to change it! Go for your dreams! It's never too late to start over. There are no excuses. Go for it. Fight for your happiness. Only you can decide how you want to live your life.

Ask yourself everyday 'is this the life that I want to live?' Ask this question to yourself every day, everywhere, all the times that you need, until you find the right answer: that only YOU know.

And even though Farouk has caused me a lot of pain, I've forgiven him. You need to forgive and leave your past to be in this moment, in the present, and continue your life with no pain, no fears, and live in faith.

And well, I'm a real love believer and I know that my McDreamy will arrive!

ABOUT THE AUTHOR

Laura Buxo, born 25th January 1980 in Spain.

She is a Finance Director and also a Bestselling Co-Author thanks to her participation in Love Unboxed Book One.

She is an expert in body language, and according to her, it is amazing what people say without talking! Laura suffered a period of intense bullying in school, which affected her self-esteem. In 2013, she married an Egyptian. It should have been her perfect love story, but in reality, he inflicted systematic psychological abuse. Now, she is divorced.

Laura is now taking her first steps as a mentor.

CONTACT

Facebook: https://goo.gl/DRWddM
Email: writetolaurabuxo@outlook.com

CONCLUSION

When the idea of this book was shared. We had an incredible response of approval from women in the Unleashed Women Community on Facebook. It was an indication that the Love Unboxed Project was timely and needed.

Not many women are courageous enough to share their untold stories to help others find answers. Understand that the purpose is not to share pain, but to inspire you to look within and find answers for yourself.

I do not know the events that has transpired in your life till this day. I learned many years back that, *the day you wake up, is a new day.* May today be your day of realisation. May nothing stop you from being the very best you can be. LIVE YOUR BEST LIFE NO MATTER WHAT.

Join us to transform the world. How? If this book has been a blessing to you, if you have been inspired by the content and you know of someone who needs to read these life stories, please share this book with them. Even better, get it as a gift. So many are dying in silence. We can change that. And you can help us.

Finally, I am very happy to share that the release of the Love Unboxed Book Series inspired the launch of The WLA Summit and Awards which held on 10th November 2017.

Here are a few photographs of the Love Unboxed Women in London UK at The WLA Awards.

AN ANTHOLOGY BY WOMEN FOR WOMEN

If you have any questions, please do not hesitate to reach out. I look forward to hearing from you. Remember,

Life is the first gift, love is the second, and understanding the third. - Marge Piercy

Life is a progress, and not a station. - Ralph Waldo Emerson

Make today and the rest of your years the best they can be. The only thing that can stop you from living life to the full is YOU!

Thank you.

Placida

ABOUT THE PUBLISHER

Placida Acheru, founder of Unleashed Women's, is a top UK Business Transformation Coach, Multi-award winning Business Growth Strategist, Multi-Time #1 Bestselling Author. She is dedicated to guiding others toward taking charge of their lives, breaking through roadblocks to systematically transform their everyday into the power to create wealth.

Placida uses her own powerful story of how she has overcome significant personal obstacles to encourage and motivate others. She is a straight-talking Business Coach, who educates clients to become laser focused on their goals. She has empowered thousands of business owners across the globe to become independent, gain visibility, credibility, growing a tribe by over 250% to generate sustainable income streams.

Her reputation has attracted the attention of the media who have invited Placida to feature in publications and events such as digital prints (www.people.co.uk), NHS Conferences and TV shows (Sky 182 Ben TV, OH TV and The Sporah Show). She was also listed in the Top 100 Most Influential Black People on digital social media drawn by eelanmedia.com.

Since embarking on a career to help and guide others, Placida Acheru has received the Inspirational Woman of the Year Award 2017, Author of the Year Award 2017, The Star Award 2017 for women making a difference, The Christian Woman in Business Award 201, Best Mentor/Coach by CA Hub Award and Professional Recognition Award 2017 by BBI Enterprise Minds.

Placida also volunteer and support several charities including Sicklecell Society, Water aid and Crisis at Christmas.

Too often the vision we hold for ourselves and our lives refuse to become reality. Visualising the life you desire and finding the journey to achieve it can seem impossible. Placida is a renowned expert to coach you through a process of self-discovery.

Other events and programs by Placida are Vision Activation Workshop, Woman Unleash Your Potential Tele-summit and WLA Book Projects

CONNECT WITH PLACIDA

Twitter: https://twitter.com/Placida_Acheru

BOOK PROJECTS.UK

On 6th January 2015, I woke up to find myself in a hospital surrounded by machines bleeping, wires attached to my body and concerned faces starring down at me. "Hello, Placida. Welcome to 2015!" I was confused. Surely it was 2014. That was my last memory. It was explained I had been in a coma for 24 days after my body reacted badly to an energy drink I sipped. This is a true story.

Still heavy dependent on the strong painkilling drugs and then having to go through the fight to ween my body off them, it took another 20 days until I could walk out of the Royal London with the aid of a frame.

As I gradually became aware of what had happened to me. "I hit me like a thunderbolt, this could have been it" buried and gone forever. I never wrote my books. Oh, my God!   All those ideas, the scribbles, the women I want to help? Have I really served? That experienced changed my focus and my business.

As humans, we carry a lot of information in the suitcase called "Experience", this information can save a life. Many have gone and never shared their life transforming stories. I have always been one who loved to listen, I love the elderly, there is so much inside of them. I love to watch people walk by and trust me I could sit all day studying and learning. When we write, we heal, we grow, we discover, and we become who we were born to be. This is the reason, I created WLA Book Projects to support women to write and explore. I bring a decade of business coaching experience into the projects. The women come to write a book, they leave with an expanded mindset and the continual support of other inspirational women.

The Whole Life Activation (WLA) Book Projects encourages building a supportive network, sharing stories and offering resources for lifestyle and business growth. More about our publishing and marketing service can be found at: http://bookprojects.uk/

Life goes far beyond us. We create legacies. Masterpieces that we can be proud to hand out to future generations. – Placida Acheru

LOVE UNBOXED BOOK ONE

AVAILABLE ON MAJOR ONLINE BOOKSTORES

DO YOU HAVE A STORY?

Have you considered writing a book? You could become an author in Love Unboxed Book 3.

Join this movement of women educating, inspiring and motivating the Next Woman to step out of fear and shame.

Let your voice be heard not to despise but to build generation next.

Visit our website for more information: http://loveunboxed.com/

Did you love this book? Got some aha! Moments?

Maybe you found yourself within its pages?

Share with us on twitter. #LoveUnboxed

Follow @LoveUnboxed @Book_Projects @womanpotentials

We would love to read your reviews.

THANK YOU.

www.ingramcontent.com/pod-product-compliance
Lightning Source LLC
Chambersburg PA
CBHW031315160426
43196CB00007B/536